CREATING A HOME

# CHOOSING A
# COLOUR SCHEME

WARD LOCK

# CONTENTS

© Ward Lock Limited, 1988
Artillery House, Artillery Row, London SW1P 1RT, a Cassell Company

Based on *Creating a Home*,
First Edition © Eaglemoss Publications Limited, 1986.

ISBN 0 7063 6726 X

Printed in Great Britain by Cooper Clegg Limited

# INTRODUCTION

With this book as your guide, you can plan colourful and imaginative decorating schemes for your home with all the confidence and flair of a professional interior designer. Forget about safe decorating schemes and dull furnishings. Armed with a basic knowledge of how colour, light, pattern and texture work together, you can create exciting and adventurous schemes with no fear of making expensive mistakes.

**Choosing A Colour Scheme** is packed with colour photographs showing dozens of different room schemes, with captions explaining what makes them work. Colour drawings demonstrate how different approaches can make the same room look radically different. And numerous colour photographs of wallcovering, fabric and floorcovering swatches show in detail what has been used in the main picture, or demonstrate the effect of putting particular colours and patterns together.

The first chapters cover the basic principles of working with colour, and explain such mysteries as using a colour wheel and how to build up a sample board. Plus, the ultimate professional touch: designing each room so that it is visually continuous with the next.

Next it is demonstrated how to create three distinctly different types of scheme: those based on harmonious colours; those based on contrasting colours; and neutral schemes enlivened with accent colours. Further chapters explain the practical aspects of colour: how it can make rooms seem large or small, light or dark, warm or cool. And a series of photographs demonstrates how the same colours change when seen in daylight and artificial lighting.

How to pick patterns is treated in the same practical way, with pages of full colour illustrations to make the points. These show how to analyse different types of pattern, how to co-ordinate patterns with colours, how to use mini prints and how to mix and match patterns and the final section covers the third design element: textures.

**Choosing A Colour Scheme** is an invaluable ideas book to use every time you plan a new decorating scheme.

# THREE WAYS TO COLOUR SCHEME

## Does choosing a colour scheme pose problems? Here are three ways to help you get it right.

Colour is probably the most useful of all the tools at the decorator's disposal. Handled properly, it can make a small room seem larger, a dark room lighter, or bring about a complete change of atmosphere.

Whether you're creating a colour scheme from scratch or updating an existing one, it's important to plan it properly. Take your time, get ideas from other people's colour schemes — in homes, offices or even restaurants — and make a note of those colours that you find satisfying and pleasing.

Before you commit yourself to a particular colour, sit down and work out what kind of look you are aiming to achieve. Start by defining the mood you want to convey — it might be warm and cosy, cool and airy, bright and cheerful, restful, pretty or stylish. Then think of which colours convey that mood. For example, warm pinks and reds create a cosy atmosphere, while cool pastels and whites give an airy, spacious feel.

Choosing colours and putting them together is partly a matter of taste, although there are general guidelines that can prove helpful.

First of all, *colours look different in different types of light.* A red which has a distinctly blue tinge in a showroom under strip lights may lose its blueness and appear a warm clear red when seen in a sunny room. A rich blue used in a dark room will appear even richer, but that same blue used in a brightly lit room can lose much of its intensity. So it is important to try out a large sample of the colour in the room in which it will be used.

Secondly, *a colour affects the colours next to it.* You may adore a certain pink and a certain green, but together they might prove disastrous. On the other hand, you may find a grey or beige dull on its own, but exactly right partnered with a lively splash of bright pink or orange.

This leads directly to the third point: *how much there is of a colour affects how you see it.* An entire room of bright pink or orange may be hard to live with, but small concentrations of those colours can make an all-white room 'sing'.

If you find choosing colours and patterns a little confusing — and most of us do — on the following five pages you will find three approaches to colour scheming, each using a different starting point.

### Match making
*There may be furniture, carpets or curtains already in the room you want to decorate, so use them as a starting point. The decorative scheme shown on the next page is based on this carpet sample.*

**The 'theme' scheme**
*The room above has a predominantly blue scheme but there are other colours used, all derived from samples assembled around the blue theme.*

*Most of the wall-coverings and fabrics here are dappled or textured for added interest and to counteract the cold quality that flat blue paint sometimes has.*

*Note how lighting affects the colours – the spotlights in this room make the colours less bright than the samples seen in daylight conditions (opposite).*

## POINTS OF DEPARTURE
Few of us have the luxury of being able to create a room scheme from scratch. You may be stuck with a major investment that can't be changed easily – a carpet or sofa, say – around which you have to plan. This can be turned to advantage, though, because it gives you a starting point from which to work. Indeed, overcoming limitations can be a greater spur to creativity!

**Collecting samples** One way to avoid expensive mistakes is to try out your chosen colours and patterns by collecting samples – like those opposite – so that you can see how they work together. Start by finding a sample of the fixture you can't change (if you can't find an exact match for your own carpet, for example, look out for one that's close to it in colour and texture).

Now start collecting scraps of fabrics, wallpaper, coloured wools and so on, in the colours you want to combine with your 'permanent fixture'. (You will find that it helps if one or two of the samples incorporate a bit of the 'fixture' colour to help tie it all together.) The current trend for co-ordinated ranges of fabrics, papers and borders makes this all much easier and more successful. You'll also be able to see whether the amount of

pattern is appealing, or too busy.

**Mix and match** Don't restrict yourself only to one range of tones. A room with light apricot walls, mid-apricot furniture and a dark apricot carpet may match perfectly, but it is also in danger of looking dull and flat. With imagination, any colour can be interpreted in many different ways. Blue, for example, can be 'true blue', blue-green or blue-violet – it can also be light or dark, pale or intense.

Subtle patterns mix and match more easily than strong, large-scale ones. Here mini-pattern and Berber weave carpets meet the practical need for a carpet

pattern without being too dominant.

The texture of a sample is also important. The blue of a cotton weave may be exactly the same as that of a shiny ceramic vase, but both 'read' differently.

Collecting samples will help you get the feel of how to vary your theme colour in interesting ways. Get together a good range of samples, then start whittling down the choice to your final selection. Finally, you can experiment with small bits of contrasting or intense accent colour to see which adds the right 'zest' that brings the whole scheme to life.

*Variations on a theme*

*When collecting samples, remember to look for different surface textures and aim to incorporate one or two accent colours, too. Here the blues and blue-greens work well with either the grey or beige carpet – but notice how touches of terracotta and the mellow maple of the picture frame bring it all to life.*

## TAKE AN EXISTING PATTERN

Professional fabric designers are expert at handling colour, so if there is a strong pattern on the carpet, walls, curtains or upholstery, follow the designer's example and use those colours as the basis for your scheme.

The colour scheme of this room (left) is based on the upholstery fabric of the sofa (right). The pale apricot background colour becomes the background colour for the walls and curtains. The cool grey-blue in the pattern is echoed in the carpet, cushions and tablecloth, while the warm terracotta is used as an accent colour in the lampshade, book bindings, table underskirt and cushion covers.

The off-white in the fabric pattern is repeated in the coffee table, shelves and panelling, to provide a welcome touch

◁ *The 'pattern' scheme*
*Taking the sofa covering as a starting point, this room's colour scheme is derived purely from the fabric pattern – apricot, grey-blue, terracotta and white.*

of freshness and stop the scheme from looking too heavy.

A pattern can tell you which colours go well together, but it can also suggest in which proportions they work best.

Look again at the picture on the left and you can see how this works in practice. The largest colour area in the pattern – apricot – is also the largest in the room. The second most dominant area, the carpet, picks up the grey-blue. Likewise, the accents of white and terracotta are used sparingly to avoid overpowering the main colours. Proportion is an exercise in subtlety and colour patterns will give you the key to a successful scheme.

By choosing such a harmonious blend of colours and tones, the owner has created a room which is elegant, restful and easy on the eye.

*Notice, too, that the colours are used in similar proportions: the apricot is the main colour and the grey-blue the secondary one, while others act as accents (right).*

## BRIGHT IDEA

### COLOUR CUES

Use patterned fabric as a guide when deciding where and how much of each colour to use in a room.

Work out roughly how much of each colour is used in the pattern – the largest areas of colour, right down to small accent colours. Now list the parts of the room to be 'coloured',

from the largest areas, walls and floor, to small accessories.

But don't stick too rigidly to the proportion idea. The dominant colours will depend on the room's size and available light: a dark colour on the walls may not be advisable in a small room, for instance.

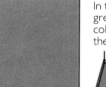

In the fabric, mid-green is the main colour; **carpet** is the largest area.

Pale green is the next main colour; **walls** are another main surface area.

The 'key' fabric used for the **curtains**, ties the scheme together.

Pale wooden **furniture** echoes the pale browns in the fabric.

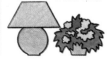
Brightest colours in the fabric are used as accent colours in **lamps, vases** and **cushions**.

A pale, muted blue is used on the **bedspread**.

### Finding inspiration

*Cut out and collect pictures of rooms that you find appealing; this way, you can pinpoint which colours you feel comfortable with and use them as a basis for creating your own colour schemes.*

*The gold and apricot tones of the magazine photographs (left) were the inspiration for the bedroom scheme (above). Soft yellow walls, an apricot carpet and creamy lace curtains create a warm, mellow mood, enhanced by subtle accents of clear pink and off-white.*

## FIND YOUR PREFERRED COLOURS

You may subconsciously have a favourite colour or colour scheme but be unable to put it into words. Or perhaps you are confused by the vast choice of decorating colours.

To overcome this problem, borrow as many interior decorating books and magazines as possible. It doesn't matter if some are out of date, or don't feature many examples of the type of room you're planning to decorate, so long as they contain plenty of colour pictures.

Quickly thumb through them all, ignoring the style of the particular rooms, but marking the colour schemes of those that appeal to you. When you've finished, put the whole lot away and out of your mind.

Return to the books and magazines you selected a week later. You may be surprised to find that most of the pictures you selected have one or more colours in common and that frequently those colours are used in a similar way. By pinpointing your preferences, you can use this information to plan your ideal colour scheme.

Remember that colours you may like to wear are not necessarily colours you can live in!

# THE LANGUAGE OF COLOUR

## Understanding colour will give you the confidence to create successful colour schemes.

Different colour schemes can make the same room seem cosy or elegant, soothing, stimulating, dramatic, even playful – and can even appear to alter the room's proportions. But, perhaps because there are so many choices, it is often hard to know where to start.

The way professional designers talk about colour can make it sound very complicated. But once you understand the basic principles of colour theory, you'll be able to create colour schemes with confidence and achieve exactly the mood and effect you want.

### THE COLOUR WHEEL
It is said that the human eye can distinguish over 10 million different colours. But every single one is based on the colours of the rainbow – red, yellow, orange, green, blue, indigo and violet – plus black and white.

To show how these basic colours relate to each other and how they combine to make all the other colours, scientists have come up with the colour wheel.

**Primary colours** The three key colours are pure red, pure yellow and pure blue. They are known as primaries, because you cannot mix them from other colours. All other pure colours can be mixed from primaries.

**Secondary colours** Orange, green and violet are mixed from equal amounts of two primaries. In between come any number of intermediate colours – dozens of different yellow-greens, blue-greens, blue-violets and so on – all mixed from their neighbour colours.

**Contrast colours** Colours that contrast most strongly are directly opposite each other on the wheel – red and green, yellow-orange and blue-violet, for example.

**Harmonious colours** These lie next to each other on the wheel. They share a common base colour – for example yellow-orange, orange and red-orange all have the colour orange in common.

**Pastels, shades and mixtures** The colour wheel is shown in pure colours (ie colours that are created from a mixture of only two neighbouring colours). But of course fabrics and paints and carpets also come paler (less intense) or lighter (with a mixture of white, known commonly as pastel). They come 'muted' or 'shaded' – with a mixture of grey or black. Or they come in subtle mixtures where a hint of colour from another part of the wheel is added – yellow-orange with a touch of blue, or a hint of red added to yellow-green.

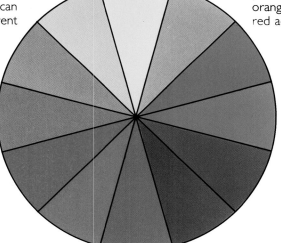

▷ **The colour wheel**
*The wheel is a useful tool for understanding how colours relate to each other and how to combine them in colour schemes.*

▽ **Secondary colours**
*Pure green is made from equal amounts of yellow and blue; violet from red and blue; and orange from red and yellow.*

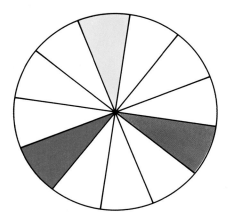

△ **Primary colours**
*The colour wheel shows how primary colours – pure red, yellow and blue – divide the wheel into three equal parts.*

## Warm colours

Reds, pinks, oranges, yellows – the colours associated with sunshine and firelight – create a cosy, welcoming atmosphere. Choose these warm colours – on the left-hand side of the colour wheel – to make a large room look smaller and friendlier, to brighten up a sunless room, or simply because you want a warm effect.

Warm peach walls, pink patterned curtains, rusty red tones in the carpet and a mass of cushions in pinks, reds and yellows set the scene in this cheerful living room. The touches of white and the cool green foliage of the plants help to balance the warm colours and prevent them from becoming overpowering.

When planning a warm scheme remember that the closer the colour is to a 'warm' primary (red or yellow), the stronger it is. Large amounts of such colours can be hard to live with, so it's often wiser to choose their softer cousins, such as pink, peach and primrose yellow, reserving the stronger colours for accents only.

## Cool colours

The other half of the colour wheel is made up of greens, blue-greens and blues – the colours of cool water and shady forests, azure skies and dappled meadows. These are the colours to use if you want a room to have a cool, calm atmosphere.

The living room shown here has a distinctly tropical flavour: the various shades of cool blue used on the walls and seat coverings evoke the sea and the sky, and are perfectly complemented by the pale, sandy colours of the furniture and flooring, while the plants add accents of lush green.

Cool colours always appear further away than warm ones. That's why cool colours make a small room appear more spacious, by 'pushing back' the walls. Be careful, however, if the room faces away from the light – cool colours here could look too bleak. Rooms that benefit from a lot of natural light can take almost any of the cool colours without appearing cold.

## Contrasting colours

You can brighten up a room by using a contrasting scheme which features colours opposite each other on the wheel – for example, red and green, or blue and orange. These pairs of colours are known as 'complementaries'. When placed close together, they intensify each other, and the result is lively and vibrant.

In this room scheme the colours have been chosen to create a cheerful, sunny effect. Contrasting colours – red and green, blue and yellow – appear in the wallpaper, paintwork and furnishings. The use of white is refreshing and accentuates the bright colours.

Contrasting colours used in equal amounts tend to produce an uneasy effect because they compete with each other, so make sure that one colour dominates. Here, the yellow sofa provides a focal point which pulls the whole room together. The green area of window is smaller, while red is only used in small touches.

## Harmonious colours

If you pick two, three or four colours that lie next to each other on the colour wheel, you can be sure that they will combine comfortably because they are closely related.

Examples of harmonious groups of colours include pink, apricot, peach and gold – or clear blues, blue-green, aqua and green – or bluebell blue, mauve and heathery purple. They work together because nothing clashes or dominates and there is a common theme between one colour and the next.

The room scheme on the left dispels the myth that 'blue and green should never be seen'. Fresh minty greens, blue-greens and emerald greens are layered upon one another, with the colours of the room echoed in accessories such as the lamp and vases.

The reds and yellows in the sofa fabric provide a touch of warmth to offset the cool effect created by the greens and blues; a small accent of contrasting colour like this is a clever way to add pep to a harmonious scheme.

### Pastel colours

Pure colours lightened with a lot of
white are known as pastels. For
example, red lightened with white
becomes pink, pure green becomes
apple green, orange becomes apricot.

These soft, gentle colours –
sometimes called 'ice-cream' or
'sugared almond' hues – are always
popular, since they look so fresh and
pretty. They blend effortlessly with the
lighter range of muted colours and with
modern and traditional styles of
furnishing. It is also interesting to note
that any pastel colour will coordinate
with another – even opposites on the
colour wheel. This is because all the
colours have a common element in that
they contain a lot of white.

The light, airy and romantic style of
this living room is achieved through the
generous use of fabrics in pale blues,
greens and mauves. Notice how several
different patterns combine without
clashing, because they're all pastels.

### Subtle and muted colours

Pure colours which are darkened with
black or grey are known as 'shades' or
'muted colours'. Then there are the
more subtle colours which are a
mixture of two or more pure colours –
for example, orange with a bit of blue.
But there is nothing dull about colours
with such evocative names as russet
brown, mustard yellow, sage green,
petrol blue, or 'crushed berry' reds such
as plum, mulberry and blackberry.
Think, too, of the rich, exuberant
lacquer colours inspired by the East –
crimson, emerald green and gold.

Here muted colours create a cosy,
autumnal feel. A variety of subtle and
muted colours is used – warm pinks,
browns and terracottas offset by cool
greens and blues.

Since muted colours contain an
element of black, they look particularly
striking when teamed with black
accents. However, you also need to
introduce a sprinkling of brighter
colours, to prevent the scheme from
becoming too heavy.

## Neutrals

In the home designer's terms, neutrals range from white, through to creams, beiges, tans and browns, and from the palest silver grey through to black. They are useful for combining with more definite colours and you can also use them to create all-neutral schemes.

Inspiration for neutral schemes can be found in the earth colours of nature. Think of the bleached white of sand, the soft browns and tans of earth and wood, and the yellowed white of ripening corn.

The group of neutral-coloured textiles shown here echoes the colours and textures of natural objects such as shells and pebbles, marble and wood. Textures and surfaces play an important part in any neutral scheme, since they add variety and interest.

Neutral colours are easy to live with, and provide a perfect foil for interesting furniture, pictures or plants.

## Tones

When you're decorating a room, it's important to think about the range of tones. Tone describes the lightness or darkness of a colour, as illustrated by these pink, red and maroon samples in light, medium and dark tones.

A room containing only light and dark tones can look disjointed and 'bitty' – so remember to include some mid-tones to link the lights and darks and give the scheme more flow. (In the group of samples, see how deeper pinks and muted reds link the very pale pinks and maroons).

To understand how tone works, think of a black and white photograph, where colours are converted into black, white and grey tones. Now imagine a room decorated entirely in light-toned colours. Boring and bland, it would photograph virtually as the same shade of grey. By using a range of tones – whatever the colours – a room scheme becomes more satisfying.

## ACCENT COLOURS

It's amazing how small touches of bright and contrasting colour bring a room to life. Most colour schemes – particularly ones based on neutrals – benefit from the addition of an accent colour. Accents need to be handled carefully though: two or three patches, not a dozen. Otherwise the effect becomes spotty.

### Contrast accents

*A room that is predominantly one colour (monochromatic) needs a few accents to add pep and interest. The colour wheel provides a handy, at-a-glance guide to choosing appropriate contrast colours – simply pick one (in this case, blue) from the side opposite the dominant colour (yellow).*

### Sharp or bright accents

*When the scheme is based on a pattern printed in several colours, it's usually effective to pick one colour, then go for touches of a brighter or more intense version of that colour. In this scheme, bright pink piping on the curtains and table mats gives style and zest.*

# WHOLE HOUSE COLOUR SCHEMES

When faced with four or five rooms to decorate and furnish at once, visual continuity is the secret of success.

*Colour inspiration*

*This hallway is painted in three very pale colours which subtly introduce you to the rest of the house. First, the cream walls create a perfect foil to the stripped pine floorboards and oriental rug. The ceiling arches and radiators are picked out in palest green, the colour carried through into the rooms leading off the hall. The ceiling is palest lavender which again could be echoed in a neighbouring room. White cornices and wood tie the scheme together.*

Professional interior designers consider visual unity very important. Experience enables them to see the whole of a house interior as one inter-related, complete decorating unit rather than a series of separate rooms. Viewing in this way helps avoid 'bittiness' and lack of continuity.

In smaller homes where space and light are usually at a premium, creating a light, neutral-coloured background using different shades of white, cream, beige and grey in walls, woodwork and flooring always work well. Any strong colour can then be added as accents with rugs and accessories. These items can easily be changed to give a neutral colour scheme a new look later on.

## LINKING – WITH FLOORING

Visual continuity and a feeling of space can be achieved by using the same or similar colour floorings throughout a home. Your choice of floorcoverings do not all have to be exactly the same material or colour to produce an effect of continuity. For instance, a honey or tan miniprint carpet in the hall and on the stairs works well with, perhaps, slightly darker floor tiles in the kitchen and a toning plain caramel carpet or stripped floorboards in the living room.

Again, when it comes to floorcoverings for the whole house, neutral colours such as beige, grey and cream work very successfully because they allow a wide choice of decoration. Choosing a light shade for a floorcovering was once considered hopelessly impractical, but with some of today's new materials this no longer applies. Modern off-white and cream textured vinyls, for example, can be extremely hardwearing and perfect for brightening a dark hallway or kitchen.

A few well-chosen rugs in similar patterns and colours can also link different flooring areas throughout a home by leading the eye through. Oriental rugs in rich colours, dhurries in pastel shades, or strong geometric art deco design rugs in neutral colours can usefully echo and link colours in several room schemes.

▽ *Floor plan*
*Each room on this plan echoes some of the colours in the adjacent room. Although the flooring is in different materials, these are linked by the same shade of grey. However, other colour links are more subtle.*

## FLOORING ALTERNATIVES

Carpet tiles are well worth considering. There are some most attractive neutral colour combinations such as grey/cream or beige/cream. Border effects can be created which also help to lead the eye through from one room to another. In common with other types of tile, damaged carpet tiles can also be easily taken up and replaced.

Some carpet tile ranges are also available with matching carpet. This is particularly useful in open-plan living/ dining arrangements where you want the same flooring all the way through from the living room to the dining room. In this case, carpet tiles are a

sensible choice in the dining area as floors here are especially vulnerable to spills and stains.

Patterned floorcoverings in neutral colours are a good compromise if you want to break up large expanses of floor and yet at the same time don't want anything too obtrusive. There is a lot of choice now in two-tone fleck, dogtooth checks, small geometric designs and stripes available in both hard and soft floorings.

Some of the newer carpet ranges have small all-over patterns in light or mid-tone colourways that suit smaller homes particularly well.

## FLOORING THRESHOLDS

There is one unfortunate snag with the brass and aluminium carpet threshold plates that hold the carpet edges firmly in place in doorways: they can detract from the overall feeling of continuity. There are wooden threshold plates that suit some interior schemes and are also less obtrusive. These can be stained, polished, or painted to blend exactly with a floorcovering.

## LINKING – WITH WALL COLOURS AND ACCENTS

The simplest way to handle all the different colours in rooms that lead off a hall or landing is to pick several different shades of the same colour. In this way they harmonize without appearing bland.

First, decide on the mood and whether you want it warm or cool. Magnolia, maize and deep egg-yolk yellow in rooms off a pale cream-painted hall or landing work well together and would give a warm effect. Pale blues, greys and lavender, on the other hand, would give a soft, cool feeling.

Accents in pictures, lighting and accessories also help to lead the eye through from one room to another. The eye will focus on any brilliant, primary coloured accents in an all-neutral scheme.

For instance, a slight touch of red in the framed print of the black and white living room opposite has been repeated in the framed prints in the hallway, red flowers on the dining room table and kitchen accessories. Small touches of red are also echoed in the red enamelled basin taps and striped blind.

▽ *Fabrics, wallpapers and carpet*
*These fabrics and co-ordinating wallpapers sparked off the whole downstairs colour scheme. A mid grey carpet is a practical 'through' colour, while touches of bright red in accessories and pictures lead the eye through to the dining area and kitchen.*

△ *Dramatic black and white*
*Inspired by the wallcoverings and fabrics of the living room, the whole house has been planned from this black and white theme leading through to sunny yellows, creams and turquoise. A mid grey flooring is a good versatile colour that can take a wide range of accents.*

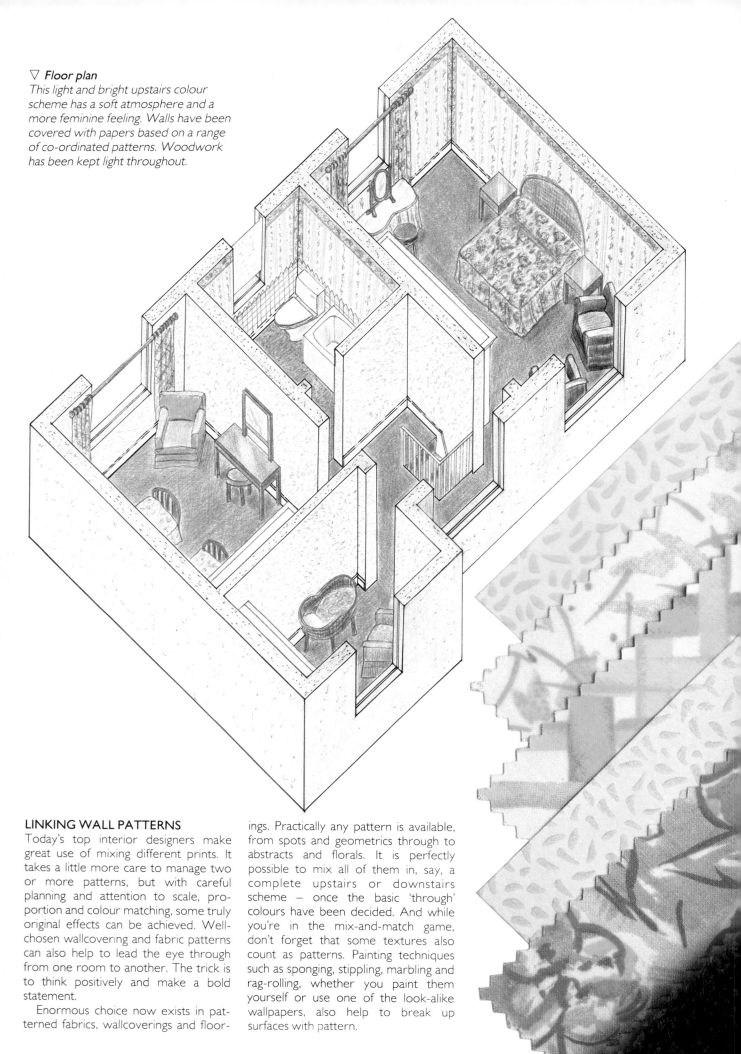

▽ **Floor plan**
This light and bright upstairs colour
scheme has a soft atmosphere and a
more feminine feeling. Walls have been
covered with papers based on a range
of co-ordinated patterns. Woodwork
has been kept light throughout.

## LINKING WALL PATTERNS

Today's top interior designers make
great use of mixing different prints. It
takes a little more care to manage two
or more patterns, but with careful
planning and attention to scale, proportion and colour matching, some truly
original effects can be achieved. Well-
chosen wallcovering and fabric patterns
can also help to lead the eye through
from one room to another. The trick is
to think positively and make a bold
statement.

Enormous choice now exists in patterned fabrics, wallcoverings and floorings. Practically any pattern is available,
from spots and geometrics through to
abstracts and florals. It is perfectly
possible to mix all of them in, say, a
complete upstairs or downstairs
scheme – once the basic 'through'
colours have been decided. And while
you're in the mix-and-match game,
don't forget that some textures also
count as patterns. Painting techniques
such as sponging, stippling, marbling and
rag-rolling, whether you paint them
yourself or use one of the look-alike
wallpapers, also help to break up
surfaces with pattern.

## SCHEMING WITH PATTERNS

Patterns can make large rooms feel cosier but too many in a small room can be claustrophobic. An interesting border with complementary paper and fabric is more effective.

When colour scheming for adjoining rooms, first choose a pattern. In this case, the bathroom wallpaper and frieze inspired the whole upstairs colour scheme. It is a good idea to isolate the colours in the most dominant pattern and build your colour scheme on these. Work in natural daylight as it is difficult to achieve good results in artificial light.

The four rooms and landing in the floor plan opposite are all colour-schemed using a number of co-ordinating papers and borders. The apricot and blue in the bathroom frieze, for instance, are picked out in the spare bedroom's apricot and blue floral wallpapers and co-ordinating fabric. A muted green carpet emphasizes the greens in the frieze.

△ *Rosebud stripe*
*This bathroom with co-ordinated wallpaper, frieze and tiles inspired the entire upstairs colour scheme. All the elements are shown in the sample board below.*

## COLOUR INSPIRATION

When visualizing a hall or landing colour scheme it helps to leave all the doors leading to the adjoining rooms open. You can then see how the hallway and landing walls act as a 'frame' for any rooms off. Instead of creamy-yellow and grey, grey walls and white woodwork in the hall below would look equally good and could lead into cooler neighbouring pale blue-grey and white rooms. For a warmer scheme the framed poster offers further inspiration: picking out the orange, for example, could successfully lead through to adjoining rooms painted in warmer peach and apricot.

Where woodwork is changing colour from one room to the next you are faced with painting the two sides of a door in different colours. Care needs to be taken in deciding exactly where one colour should end and the other begin. When the door is closed all is well, but when the door is open you'll see the edges as well. It works best to paint the opening edge of the door the same colour as the face which opens into the room and the hinged edge to match the other face. This way, when the door is left open, the colour of the visible edge and the face of the door are continuous from whichever room they are viewed.

▽ *Dramatic deco*
*Black, cream and grey in this hall carpet and dramatic geometric deco rug team beautifully with cream walls, pale grey woodwork and natural ash furniture.*

# HANDLING SAMPLES SUCCESSFULLY

Samples – and a well-planned sample board – are the key to working out a colour scheme that turns out the way you want.

The prospect of putting a room scheme together – choosing colours for walls, curtains, floor and wall coverings – is exciting. But with so many possibilities to choose from it's hard to know where to start.

That's where samples come in. By collecting a variety of samples – a mixture of plains, patterns and textures, wallpapers, paint charts, carpets and fabrics – you can make sure the colour scheme is successful.

First you need a starting point of some kind. It could be a sofa, a carpet or some curtains you have already, or perhaps just an idea of the effect you want – warm and lively, for instance, or calm and harmonious. The colour wheel (see The Language of Colour) is a useful tool to help you identify the colours that work with your sofa or carpet, or that create the effect you're after.

Play with the samples in different groupings. Once you have decided what goes well together take it a step further and make up a sample board like interior designers do. This way, all the swatches of fabric, wallpaper, carpet and paint can be seen together in roughly the proportions they will be used. Then you can start to see in your mind's eye what the finished room will look like.

Finally, allow time for decisions. Impulse buys are usually the ones you regret later. Keep the sample board in the room for a few days to see how you feel about each element after the first flush of enthusiasm wears off.

◁ *Patterns*
*There is an enormous choice available – floral and geometric, abstract and traditional. Small patterns may lose definition in a large room, while big patterns can overpower a small room.*

◁ *Plains*
*Plain paint, carpets, or fabrics such as cottons and velvets help to set off patterns and textures.*

▷ *Textures*
*Texture describes how a material appeals to the sense of touch – rough or smooth, ribbed or velvety. Fabrics and wallcoverings are also printed to look like textures – spattered, wood grain, watered silk and other tactile effects.*

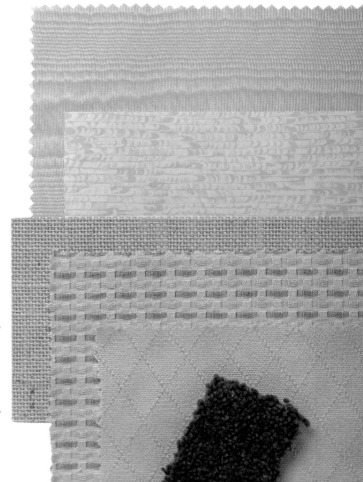

## PLANNING AROUND A PATTERN

The starting point can be any existing pattern on a sofa, a carpet, curtains, wallpaper, even a cushion. This will provide the key to your colour scheme – and your collection of samples.

Begin by identifying the different colours in the pattern and then select two or three to become the basis for the scheme.

Collect the samples in a variety of plains, patterns and textures, so you have plenty of choice. Plains do not always provide enough visual interest and patterns can sometimes be too much, so it's important to consider textures too.

**Collecting the samples** It is always better to choose from samples of the actual items – a square of carpet, for example, or a swatch of fabric – rather than from printed images in catalogues which may be different colours from the real thing. If you are designing a room around beiges, for instance, a carpet that turns out slightly pinker than the printed sample could spoil the whole scheme.

**Handling patterns** It is always difficult to imagine what a finished scheme will look like on the basis of tiny samples. So with large-patterned wallpaper or fabric, try to get a large sample.

Look at the photos in pattern books to help you imagine the overall effect and whether, in quantity, it will be pleasing or overbearing. If in doubt, it's better to buy one roll first rather than put up with long-term disappointment.

**Handling paint** In the same way, it is difficult to imagine what a whole room painted in a colour chosen from a paint chart will look like. You need to see the colour on its own, not as a tiny patch surrounded by other similar colours.

Once you've narrowed your choice down to one or two colours, it's a good idea to buy a small pot of each and try them out in the room – but remember that wet paint usually dries a shade or two darker. If you paint on to a large sheet of cardboard, you can see how the colour looks by different pieces of furniture, in the sun, or in a dark corner.

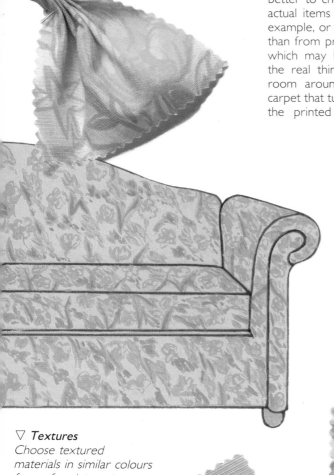

▽ *The starting point*
*The sofa fabric makes a good base for the scheme because it contains so many colours.*

▷ *Plains*
*Identify the colours in the sofa fabric and collect samples of them – floor coverings and paint charts, fabrics and wallpapers.*

▽ *Patterns*
*The sofa fabric has a distinctive pattern, so choose other patterns that include the same colours. Check that pattern scales work together.*

▽ *Textures*
*Choose textured materials in similar colours for surface interest.*

## MAKING A SAMPLE BOARD

A sample board is one of the 'tricks of the trade' of professional interior designers. It helps you judge whether colours, patterns and textures work together, and gives a good idea how the scheme will look.

To make a sample board you need a piece of plain cardboard about 20cm × 30cm as a base (the grey/beige inside of a cornflakes packet will do, or a piece of white card, but keep the colour of the board neutral).

Usually about one sixth of the colour in a room comes from the floor, another sixth from curtains and upholstery, and the remaining two thirds from walls and ceiling. Try to aim for samples in these proportions so they virtually cover the board — if necessary, get two or three samples of the chosen carpet to make a large enough patch. If the floor is wood, see if you can find something to match.

Finally, try out bits of wool or paint chips to see which accents work best with the overall colour scheme.

### Using the sample board
*Left: the sample board. Below: how the room will eventually look.*

## SHOPPING HINTS

It's worth exploring specialist furnishing shops to look at pattern books with well co-ordinated ranges of wallpapers and fabrics. Even if you don't buy them, they provide ideas for what colours go together and how to mix patterns and plains.

For a small fee, some shops will supply larger samples. Or, for a returnable deposit, they will loan a metre or more.

## BRIGHT IDEA

### PATTERN HINTS
One problem in choosing a patterned wallpaper or fabric (particularly one with a large design) is imagining how it will look when it is hung. Some pattern books have photographs that show the overall effect in a room; and some shops provide a large 'viewing' mirror — an idea to copy at home.

If you stand well back and hold up the sample in front of the mirror the distance between you and the mirror is doubled, in the reflection, giving you a more objective view of how the sample will look. Some small patterns seem to 'disappear' or merge into a single colour when viewed at a distance.

To get an idea of the repeat effect, hold the sample at right angles close to the mirror: the pattern is reflected and appears twice as wide.

## THE IMPORTANCE OF LIGHTING

When choosing paints and materials, it is essential to make your selection under the same lighting conditions as those in your home – another reason why collecting samples is a good idea. You should take the samples into the room to be decorated and look at them by both daylight, and by electric light at night. Consider when you use the room most. If it's during the daytime, then make sure you choose your scheme from the samples that look best in daylight. Think about the atmosphere you want to create, too – a warm, inviting living room or a fresh, sunny bedroom, for example.

It is easy to think that all electric lights are the same. In fact, the various types of artificial lighting affect certain colours in different ways. A normal tungsten light (the kind produced by standard light bulbs) makes pale blues slightly dull and grey, while reds appear more vivid. Under a warm white fluorescent strip, purples have distinctly pink overtones, but pinks appear dull.

Colours can vary in daylight conditions too. If you look around a room by day, you'll notice how the light on one wall is slightly different from that on the wall next to it – the intensity of light depends on the position of the windows and doors, the way the house faces and the time of day.

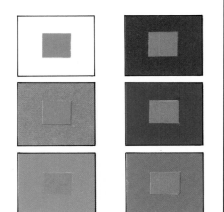

### HOW COLOURS AFFECT EACH OTHER

The red used here is the same in every illustration. See how different it looks when it's placed next to other colours.
☐ White makes it look clear and intense, black makes it lighter.
☐ Grey makes the red darker, blue makes it brighter.
☐ Next to orange – a closely related colour – the red looks darker and less true; green – the colour directly opposite on the colour wheel – makes red appear very bright.

## ONE PLAIN COLOUR – THREE DIFFERENT LOOKS

If you're starting with a plain colour – whether it's walls, carpet or upholstery – you have an almost limitless choice. So think about the kind of look you want to create – it could be elegant or cottagey, flowery or high-tech – and then choose with that in mind.

In the room schemes below the basic starting point is the toffee-coloured carpet. By mixing patterns and textures, and branching out with loosely co-ordinated colours and patterns, it is possible to create three schemes, each with a totally different feel.

The overall look of a room depends not just on colours, but also on the size and type of patterns – anything from large floral prints to small geometrical designs – and the textures of the materials used. So consider these different factors as you go about collecting samples.

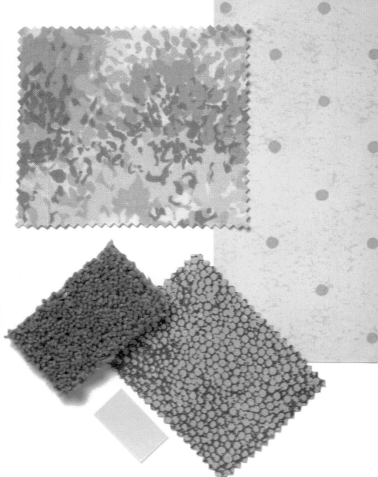

△ *Elegant and understated*
*The subtle 'texture' patterns used in the fabric and wallpaper echo the carpet texture. The colours all relate to each other, and are colours found in nature, calm and subdued. The curtains and sofa are chosen for their understated, elegant lines, and the overall effect is one of lightness.*

## △ Sophisticated fun

Here pattern is combined with pattern, spots with stripes, stripes with florals for a spontaneous and freehand look. It works because the colours are slightly muted but still lively, the patterns abstract, the textures smooth. A touch of toffee in the fabrics is just enough to unify the scheme.

## △ Cottage effect

Here, common denominator colours of sand, toffee and maroon make patterns of different scales and character work together. Sand-coloured cushions and piping break up the large area of maroon on the sofa, while the smooth wall surface offsets the woven cotton of the sofa fabric and the twist pile texture of the carpet.

## SAME SAMPLES – TWO SCHEMES

Exactly the same materials can be used to create quite different effects, depending on how you use larger and smaller patterns, lighter and darker colours.

If you can find a picture of a room that looks roughly like the one to be decorated, it's worth tracing it on to plain paper and colouring in the different areas to match the samples. This gives an idea of how a large area of china blue on walls, for example, will look as opposed to a much smaller area of the same blue used for blinds or a cushion.

▷ *Light and airy*
*The bold 'stencil-look' wallpaper pattern creates a fresh, airy look. Patterns with white backgrounds usually make rooms seem light and more spacious.*

▷ *Rich and glowing*
*For an all-over colour effect, the floral mini-print wallpaper is used. Note how the background blue predominates: coloured grounds tend to hold furnishings together, bring walls in.*

30

# HARMONIOUS COLOURS

Combine closely related colours to create harmonious schemes that are easy to live in.

Greens, blues and mauves work well together; pinks, peaches and apricots are a successful mixture, too. When you combine colours like these, which are closely related on the colour wheel, you can be certain of creating harmonious colour schemes.

The degree of harmony depends on how closely related the colours are. The colour wheel that appears on page 13 is divided into 12 sections but it could be divided into many more, with subtler differences in colour.

If you move around the colour wheel and choose any group of colours which lie near (but not necessarily adjacent to) each other, they will create a comfortable harmony. The most obvious way to divide colours is into warm and cool groups. Pinks, reds and yellows, for example, are all on the warm side; blues, greens and mauves are on the cool side. A warm harmony of colours creates an inviting atmosphere in a large or small room; and a careful combination of cool colours can create space.

## TEMPERATES

You can also make successful harmonies by mixing colours which link the warm and the cool side of the colour wheel. These are called temperate colour combinations. Orange, yellow and green, for example, are a warm temperate harmony mixing warm colours (orange and yellow) with a touch of coolness (green). Red and pink with mauve are a warm temperate combination from the other end of the range.

Yellow used with green and blue, or blue and mauve with pink, are both cool temperate colour combinations in which cool colours are warmed up with a colour from the warm side of the wheel. So, if your starting point is blue – maybe in the carpet or on the walls – and you want an harmonious scheme you can move in either direction on the colour wheel, towards a sunny yellow or a warm pink.

Harmony is even easier to create using tints and shades of just one colour – think of the hundreds of shades there are of any single colour. However, this kind of scheme often lacks life, so additions of small accents of strong or more contrasting colours, and varying textures, help to make the overall scheme more interesting.

*Natural harmony*
*Warm and cool harmonies are found in the subtle colours in nature – yellows, oranges, russets, ochres, reds and pinks; or soft blue, lilac, mauve, greens and purples.*

## WARM HARMONIES

Using a harmony of warm colours always makes a room appear inviting and comfortable. The warm range of colours stretches from scarlet through oranges, to yellow, and includes pinks, pale peaches, rich plums and ochres.

The closer a colour is to a primary such as red – the warmest and most vibrant of the warm range – the more intense the colour will be. These intense versions of warm colours are very lively and need to be carefully controlled, otherwise they can be very difficult to live with.

So, if you want to avoid a restless combination of colours, choose an harmonious scheme. Pick colours which are close together on the colour wheel, mixing pure colours with lighter and darker tones.

Remember that the strength of colours varies. The richness of autumn can be found in the darker versions of oranges and reds; the pastel equivalents are softer and fresher, and probably better suited to warming up a small cold room without being overbearing.

In this living room the apricot walls, scorched pink velvet upholstery and peach lampshade give it a warm, comfortable feel – with such a high ceiling it could easily have turned out cold and austere.

△ **Warm and welcoming**
*The warm harmony of colours in this large living room are perfectly complemented by the rich gilt of the mirror frame and the natural wood of the table and the fireplace.*

◁ **Oranges and lemons**
Yellow is a particularly useful temperate colour. It can be a warm sunny yellow with a hint of orange, or a cooler lemon, closer to green. It is also easily influenced by other colours.

  The warm yellow in this room is tempered by the apricot and soft green in the floral print of the upholstery and the blinds.

◁ **Hot pinks, cool lilacs**
Pinks from the warm range of colours are cooled with a lilac-grey in this colour scheme. The warm coral pink is mixed with a vivid pink in the upholstery fabric and the blind. The lilac walls and the pale pink of the painted wicker chair blend with the lilac-grey carpet and the grey table.

## COOL HARMONY

Blue sky and green grass – an harmonious colour scheme made in heaven. Almost any shade of blue goes with all the different greens – light blues with emerald, soft green with soft turquoise, mauve with deep green.

Interesting cool harmonies are simply created using differing amounts of several colours and by using different intensities of colour.

In the light airy bedroom above, for instance, a combination of blues with pale green creates a serene, restful atmosphere – refreshing to wake up to. The pale moss green and the lilac-grey of the carpet soften the cool crispness of the overall scheme.

In a colour scheme that is predominantly blue it seems quite natural to add a little green, a closely related cool colour, to lighten the effect.

## COOL TEMPERATES

It is often a good idea to introduce a touch of warmth to the cools. In a scheme dominated by mauve, using deep pink, a warm colour close to mauve on the colour wheel, will maintain the harmonious effect and add warmth and interest.

Similarly, at the green end of the cool range, a warm colour such as a sandy beige, could be included – in cushion or curtain fabrics, perhaps – to warm up an otherwise cool scheme.

△ *Cool companions*
*In this bedroom, which gets plenty of natural light and warmth, a combination of soft blue, mint green and lilac-grey creates a very fresh atmosphere.*

◁ *Cool alternatives*
*Colours from the other end of the cool range – blues and greens – are combined here with a soft, sandy yellow. The coolness of the blues and greens are equally balanced; although the green appears in smaller areas it is more intense. The element of warmth in the yellowish beige softens an otherwise cool scheme and adds to the airiness of the room.*

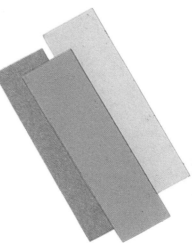

◁ *Greys and pinks*
*Here a cool harmony of blue-grey lilac is combined with deep pink.*
  *The walls below the dado rail are painted in a delicate lilac; above the rail a soft pink is sponged over white. The matching curtain and tablecloth fabric combines a broad blue-grey stripe with splashes of vivid pink, repeated in the hydrangea blooms outside.*
  *White is used to bring light and freshness into the overall scheme.*

## SINGLE HARMONY

Combining shades of just one colour is an alternative way of creating an harmonious colour scheme. Any colour you choose will have a wide range of tints and shades from the palest and freshest to the very darkest. A restful combination of greens, for instance, can include a pale jade and a deep green.

It's important to choose tones from all parts of the range so that the colour scheme works. Using a selection of shades from the dark and the light ends of the range tends to make the overall effect seem disjointed, because there are no mid-tones.

Once you've decided on the colour, it's quite straightforward to put together a single colour scheme, but it's also easy for these schemes to turn out to be monotonous. To avoid ending up with a dull lifeless room, add accents of colour in cushions or vases perhaps.

The accent colour need not be strong. However, they are most effective when they are contrast colours chosen from the opposite side of the colour wheel – red or orange with green, perhaps, or blue with yellow – but be careful not to break up the harmony by using too many.

△ *Cool and soothing*
*A simple combination of shades of jade with white creates a restful – but monotonous – atmosphere in this sunny living room.*

▽ *Strong accents*
*Accents of a bright yellow – in the lampshade, cushions and vases – are just enough to add life to the scheme.*

# WORKING WITH ACCENT COLOURS

Learn how to use touches of colour – warm or cool, subtle or bright – to bring new life to your colour schemes.

Most colour schemes are improved by the addition of accents – the final touches of colour which can make a room come alive, or complement a colour scheme. They are usually provided by accessories, such as lampshades, cushions, picture frames, towels, soaps, tablecloths, candles, flowers or blinds. Using accents successfully is straightforward once you understand a few simple rules.

## USING ACCENTS

The power of an accent colour depends on the background of colours it is combined with. If, for example, the colour scheme is dominated by a warm sandy yellow, the accent colour could come from the cool side of the colour wheel – blues or greens, perhaps – to introduce a lively contrast; a choice of red or pink accents – almost opposite yellow on the colour wheel – would be more striking.

Accents needn't be strong contrast colours to be successful. Adding accents which are closely related to the basic colour scheme has an harmonious and restful effect, and can be used to emphasize individual tones.

Don't be put off using accents if there is pattern in the room. A colour which is common to all the patterns can be picked out as an accent to provide a visual link between the various elements. A soft pastel floral wallpaper in pinks and greens combined with a plain striped sofa in a shade of green, for instance, would be perfectly complemented by a few accents in a more intense tone of the same green.

Try to avoid using the same accent colour in too many places, or too many accent colours in one room. In a living room, for example, limit the accents to three or four places, such as cushions, a lampshade or a picture frame which can be easily changed.

## NEUTRAL COLOUR SCHEMES

Accents are particularly important in monochrome or neutral colour schemes which can sometimes look dull. Try covering up the shocking pink accents in the picture on this page and see how the well-balanced neutral colour scheme of grey and white loses its impact.

Neutral colour schemes can provide a background for a mixture of different accent colours. The combination can be harmonious or contrasting depending on the effect you want to create.

*Colour power*
*This strong and plain neutral colour scheme needs splashes of a powerful colour, such as a bright vivid pink, to bring it alive.*

## CHOOSING YOUR ACCENTS

Look carefully at the contents of the room before deciding on accent colours. Upholstery fabric, paintings, posters or china are already part of the decoration scheme and often provide the inspiration. Accents are easy to change and a familiar colour scheme can be quickly given a fresh look with a new range of accents.

▷ *Quick change*
*Changing a tablecloth is an easy way to bring fresh colours into a dining room. Here, the pink candles are used as accents to draw out the red of the checked tablecloth. Blue or white candles would make good alternatives.*

▽ *Perfect link*
*Checks, stripes and miniprints are combined in this living room. The strong yellow of the lampshade acts as an accent which links all the patterns together.*

## △ Painted inspiration

The accent colours used for the cushions in this living room are taken from the painting on the left hand wall. The cream walls and furniture provide a neutral background which can, therefore, take more accent colours than a coloured room. Here five different accents are used – pink, red, green, yellow, blue – any more and the effect would be spotty. The deep blue vase on the mantelpiece echoes the painting over the fireplace.

## ▷ Blue and white

In this bedroom, white was picked out of the painting on the wall and used as the accent colour for the wall lights, skirting board and traditional fireplace surround. It makes a strong, crisp contrast with the cool blue colour scheme.

Picking out the architectural features, such as the cornice, skirting board, ceiling rose, moulding on panelled doors or fireplace surround, is another way of bringing accents into a decorating scheme.

## CONTRAST AND HARMONY

Contrasting accent colours can have a variety of effects on a colour scheme, from the strongest impact created by bringing together opposites on the colour wheel – a bright red used in a green room scheme, for instance – to subtle mixtures of pastel tones.

Harmonious accent colours are easier to use successfully. They should be close to the basic colour scheme on the colour wheel but they can be darker or lighter depending on the effect you want to create.

### △ Warm contrast
*The rich deep red in the floral curtain fabric has been picked out as a strong contrasting accent colour for the picture mounts, lampshade and cushion in this warm yellow living room.*

### ▷ Sharp accents
*Neutral colour schemes can take almost any colour as an accent. Dark grey and white provide an excellent background for strong primary yellow accents in this kitchen.*

△ **Cool harmony**
You can add interest to an harmonious colour scheme – without destroying the harmonious effect – by using stronger or lighter versions of the same or closely-related colours. In this cool blue and green living room the lampshade in jade emphasizes the more delicate tones of the marbled wallcovering and the sofa fabric.

▷ **Country colours**
In this living room the colour scheme is based on the colours in the floral upholstery fabric – soft moss green, beige and pale blue. The coffee tables are painted in a deeper shade of blue to add interest without destroying the harmonious effect. A deep green would make a good alternative accent.

## USING ACCENTS WITH NEUTRALS

Neutral colours include any shade of grey in the range of tones from white to black, as well as beiges, browns, cream and ochres. Neutral colour schemes can easily become dull and lifeless without accents; but almost any colour can be used as an accent and, to change the mood completely, simply change the accessories. In this beige scheme a variety of contrasting and harmonious accents have been added.

△ *The fine black lines of the picture frames, the lamp bases and the trim on the bedcover and cushion work well as a strong neutral accent in this bland colour scheme.*

△ *A group of drawings in deep terracotta frames set against a cream marbled wall, with matching lampshades and piping on the cushions, add a warm touch.*

△ *A neutral colour scheme needs a range of textures and accents to add visual interest. Touches of a bright colour such as yellow liven up this scheme.*

# CONTRAST COLOUR SCHEMES

Room schemes made up from contrasting colours can be strong and eye-catching or gently coloured and restful.

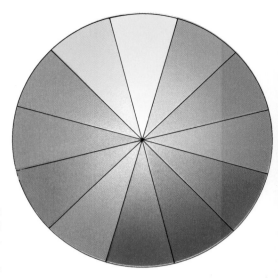

Contrast colour schemes, whether in bright or pastel tones, have one thing in common: their principal colours lie on opposite sides of the colour wheel.

They do not necessarily have to be direct opposites, but can be taken from anywhere on the opposing half of the colour wheel: with red as the parent colour, any colour from indigo to yellow ochre can be used as a contrast, or with leaf green as the parent, any shade from orange through red, pink, and violet can be used. Tonal values are important as the two main colours need to be fairly evenly balanced. The less intense the shades you choose, the easier the scheme will become: both pastel and muted shades, even when contrasting, in the end become harmonious.

Balance is important. Don't use two colours in equal quantities as they can 'intensify' each other. On the other hand, avoid the spotty effect created by just dotting the complementary colour around the scheme. At the same time, using just two colours can be sombre, so use others to act as background and accents to give the room a 'lift'. They can make the main colours more vibrant or tone them down.

△ **Graded colour wheel** *shows all the hues, from deep tones to light pastels.*

▽ *Confident contrast*
*A colour scheme carried through with confidence. Strong, grass-green walls are countered by orangey-red blinds of equal weight. The beige, orange and green carpet provides perfect balance.*

◁ *Clearly contrasting*
*The parent colour – yellow – contrasts in classic fashion with clear sky blue. The yellow is present in two hues: soft daffodil painted on the table and skirting board, sharp buttercup as accent in the teapot, cup and saucer. The creamy-beige wall and blue-beige carpet tie the colours together.*

▽ *Contrast – or harmony?*
*Pale pastel-yellow walls inset with cream panels act as the parent colour in this elegant room. A clear delft blue in the screen, tablecloths and cushions acts as a contrast. The creamy-grey carpet and upholstery form the neutral back-drop, with yellow piping and ribbons as accent. Light entering the room from the window makes the two sofas appear almost different in colour as it falls on them. The mix of pastels, while strictly complementary, is almost harmonious because they are so light in tone.*

## IMPORTANCE OF LIGHT

It's important to look at the colours in the room where they are to be used, as different light can affect colouring to a considerable degree.

If you want to use a strong colour for the walls, it is worthwhile buying a small pot of paint and painting a large sheet of card. Prop it against the wall for a few days to see the effect of different light conditions in your room. Strong colours tend to look even stronger on a large area and in a fairly small room the colour reflects from one wall to the other to intensify the effect.

Lay colour samples against each other while you consider them, not against white or a neutral, and don't put more than three intense colours to-gether. On the other hand, if you are using muted or pastel shades, you can mix any number of colours. Use pattern – in carpet, for example – to link the parent colour with complementaries.

## ▷ Classic contrast

Dark rooms with little light can take more intense colours in a contrast colour scheme because they become more muted. In this bedroom a very strong yellow – which might be overpowering in a lighter room – is used to good effect as the contrast colour against a mid-blue parent. The darker blue stencil designs on the wall and frills on the quilt, with white lampshade and frills on the canopy, act as accents. On the floor, the rug combines all the colours used and the coffee-coloured carpet acts as a neutral background.

## ▽ Colour ranges

A range of blue and yellow paint chips shows how well these two opposing colours work together in contrasting schemes.

### △ Geometric contrast

Turquoise-painted walls and deeper-toned carpet form an all-enveloping parent colour contrasted by angular blocks of bandbox pink. A deeper-toned pink picks out the woodwork. Subtle indirect lighting hidden behind the bedhead causes interesting light-and-shadow effects on the wall above. Bed linen in the palest of pastel pinks forms the neutral relief colour.

### ◁ Three-way contrast

Three blocks of colour in almost equal weight make an exciting modern scheme in a café-style dining corner. While the yellow and turquoise are nearly the same tonal value, the deep red floor is altogether much darker. The same red, used with light navy blue, serves as accent colour in the painted border round the wall. The neutral shiny black table and chairs make the colours appear brighter.

## CONTRAST COLOUR CHART

| COLOUR | CONTRAST | ACCENTS | NEUTRALS |
|---|---|---|---|
| **RED** Scarlet / Terracotta | Emerald / Dark ivy / French navy / Bright blue | Tan/ Sand / Naples yellow/ Dusky pink | Cream/ White / Ivory/ Beige |
| **GREEN** Deep blue-green / Citrus green | Peach / Deep dusty pink / Royal blue | Light green/ Turquoise / Purple/ Lilac | Oyster/ White / Silver/ White |
| **YELLOW** | Mid-blue | Green | Yellowish white/ Green-greys |
| **BLUE** | Burnt orange | Scarlet | Blue-white/ Grey |
| **PINK** | Turquoise | Deep blue-green | Magnolia/ Blue-grey |

## BRIGHT IDEA

**Work out a scheme** You can work out an interesting contrasting colour scheme by using the standard colour wheel.

Trace over the diagram at right, then re-trace it on to card or thick paper. (Alternatively, use carbon paper to mark the diagram on to a sheet of paper underneath.) Cut out the shaded segments and pin the circle through the marked centre point on to the colour wheel printed on to page 43.

The triangular segment represents the parent colour. Turn the circle round on the wheel, depending on which colour you are planning to use as the parent, and any of the colours showing through the semi-circular window can be used as a contrast.

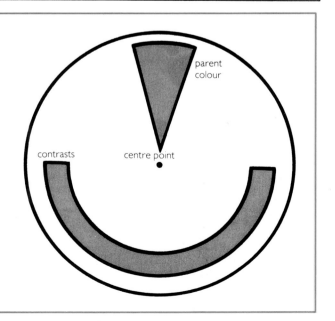

## EXPERIMENT WITH COLOUR

If you're not totally colour confident, it's sometimes a good idea to experiment with colour scheming in a smaller room, or by using paints – which are inexpensive and easy to change if you are unhappy with the results.

A bathroom, shower room, or WC (all too often unexcitingly decorated) are good places to start. You may hit upon a colour scheme that pleases you, but if not, the walls can be quickly repainted. Try using lighter or more muted shades. Don't forget to include calming neutrals and one or two accent points to obtain the complete effect.

This sort of experimentation helps to build up your confidence and enables you to create a really exciting colour scheme in the future in one of the main rooms of your home. .

△ *Holly inspiration*
The classic contrast of red and green, used here in mid-tones, gives this bathroom a cheerful aspect. Neutral white on the ceiling and painted beams add lightness and brightness.

▽ *Variations on a theme*
This bathroom with butterscotch walls contrasted by a lilac-coloured bath provides an interesting variation on a yellow-and-blue theme. The greyish-green hand-basin and tiles provide gentle accent colour, with white as the background neutral.

△ *Warming bathroom*
Rich terracotta walls give a warming glow, contrasted by the vibrant blue-painted bath exterior. Gleaming brass fittings act as accents and the neutral white ceiling lightens the whole room.

# UNDERSTANDING TONE

## If you can't put your finger on what is missing from a room scheme – it's often the tonal mix that is wrong.

Basically, 'tone' describes the lightness and darkness of a colour. Technically, the tone of a colour can be affected by two things: the *intensity* (amount) of the colour and *value* – the amount of black or white it contains. The combination of intensity and value produces the *tone*.

Whether you like muted or pastel shades, warm colours or bright contrasts, understanding tone really does help in making decisions about colours.

It also helps you to create a well-balanced scheme which is neither too bland and boring, nor too busy.

An all-over, one-colour scheme can be made visually interesting by using several different tones of that colour – from the palest pastel through to a really deep shade. Alternatively, a many-coloured, many patterned room – which might seem to be in danger of becoming a visual mess – can be saved if all the colours are closely related in tone. And when evaluating the overall tonal mix don't forget to take the tone of any woodwork into account.

To use tone successfully, it helps if you can recognise similar tones in different colours – something you are probably already doing subconsciously. Once you do understand tonal intensities and values, and how to combine them, you can create room schemes that are lively and interesting as well as satisfactorily balanced.

**How tone works** It is often hard to notice the tonal relationship of colours when looking at a coloured photograph, but in a black-and-white photograph or a film, where colours are converted into shades of grey, it is much more obvious. Good newspaper pictures and old 1940s films work because there's a good range of tonal contrast. The two photographs of the same room below – first in colour, then in black and white – clearly show the different tonal values.

◁ *Balancing the tones*
*The cheerful, multi-coloured patchwork blends harmoniously because many of the patches are of approximately the same tonal value; only the darker blue and white are different. Looking at the black and white photograph you'll notice how the darker blue tone ties in with the wood fireplace and that without the white patches the overall effect would be quite dull and lifeless.*

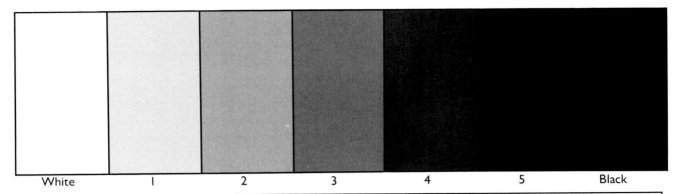

| White | 1 | 2 | 3 | 4 | 5 | Black |

## TONE SCALE

The diagram above shows seven gradations of tone ranged between pure white and pure black. The tones range from very light through a semi-light, quite light, mid-tone, quite dark to very dark. This is a simplified tone scale, and is one that can be easily distinguished by the human eye. Your eye can quickly learn to give an approximate 1-5 rating to different colours.

Below is a range of shades in three colours progressing from the lightest shade to the darkest. Comparing the colours in a line across the page you'll notice that each shade has roughly the same tonal value or intensity.

### HOW TO TEST FOR TONE

To consider the tones that are contained in a fabric design you are thinking of using, here is an experiment to try.

☐ First, match paint samples as closely as possible to the colours in the fabric.

☐ Next cut them out and then lay them out on an off-white background such as a grey or buff envelope.

☐ Then screw up your eyes and squint a little at the colours. Move them around if necessary, so that they lie next to other shades.

☐ Screw up your eyes again; if the colours seem to merge, then they are quite close together in tone. On the other hand, if they don't merge, then the colours are of quite different tones.

☐ Armed with this knowledge, you'll be able to make much more effective decisions when choosing the shades and tones of any accent colours you want to accompany your decorating scheme and enhance it to the maximum effect.

## Working with fabrics

When learning to judge tonal ranges start with a flat printed pattern so you will not be distracted by light and shadow as in a complete room.

In the photograph on this page there is a fabric designed by William Morris with a well-defined, strong pattern that contains several colours and tones. Around it are grouped together samples of plain fabrics in the same dark tones and the same pale tones that correspond to the colours in the fabric. The two main colours – pink and green – are in the same tonal range.

The differences in tonal range show up well in the black-and-white photograph. Note how the extremities of the range – the very light and the very dark tones – are used sparingly, and act as accents.

## FEW COLOURS/MANY TONES

Room schemes on a one-colour (mono-chrome) theme need not be dull. You can make them visually effective by working with a range of shades from very pale to very intense, running through the whole of the tonal range.

**Shadows** When evaluating the tonal range don't forget to take into account areas of permanent shadow, such as the folds of drapery or the shadow cast by a large wardrobe. These obviously darken the tone of any colour, adding an extra dimension to the tonal range.

▷ *One-colour schemes*
*While basically one colour, this room works well because of its wide variety of tones. Here the intensely bright ribbon hanging down over the bed lifts the whole scheme and creates immediate visual interest. White lacy cushions on the bed and white paintwork mark the opposite end of the tonal range.*

◁ *Sea-misty*
*A wide range of sea-green tones come together to create a varied but restful mood.*

▽ *The black-and-white photograph of the scene on the left clearly indicates the range of tones and how the areas of shadow created by the drapery add movement and variety to the overall scheme. The tone scale shows that every tone is included except black.*

## MANY COLOURS/FEW TONES

A room scheme that combines too many colours can look busy and restless. However, if most of the colours are as close together as possible in the tone scale this will greatly help to calm and unify the whole scheme.

### ▷ Multi-coloured schemes

*This bed-sitting room is decorated all over in rich, mid-to-dark colours – predominantly terracotta, blues and greens. There are two differently-patterned wallpapers and a paper border; and several fabric patterns. Even the ceramic lamp and paper shade have the same rich colours, as do the various cushions that are dotted round the room for accent.*

*The reason that this works as a cohesive and harmonious scheme – rather than just looking like a hotch-potch – is because, apart from the white accents outlining the paisley patterns, the colours themselves come from a narrow tonal range – as can be seen below from the black-and-white print of the lamp corner on the desk.*

### ▷ Warmth and light

*Although of quite a different colour, the mainly red lampshade blends harmoniously into the background of mainly green curtain fabric because – as can be seen from the black-and-white print – its tonal value is practically the same. In the evenings artificial light also plays a part in varying the tonal contrast, deepening shadows and highlighting the palest tones.*

# AVOIDING TONAL TRAPS

Sometimes it helps to see why schemes do *not* work, in order to understand how to avoid the obvious pitfalls. The left-hand column of drawings shows three common problems: the centre column shows the problem in black and white terms: and the right-hand column shows one way to put the tonal balance right. Now try to imagine what colours should be used to produce the tones illustrated in the third column.

Bear in mind the tonal range of wood too. Whether it is light ash, mid oak, dark mahogany or stained black will affect the overall tonal balance of a scheme, just as much as the more obvious colour differences.

**Problem: spotty and stark**
*There are lots of intense red elements, with black and white.*

**Tonal analysis** *This scheme looks virtually all black and white, because intense colours are tonally very dark.*

**Solution** *Adding a mid-tone background – either on the walls or floors – helps to link extreme tones.*

**Problem: too garish**
*This scheme includes several pastels and several intense colours.*

**Tonal analysis** *As well as a variety of colours, there is a wide range of tones from very light to very dark.*

**Solution** *To maintain a colourful scheme, it's best to stick to a narrow band of tones for the colours.*

**Problem: bland and boring**
*All the colours are slavishly picked out from the blind fabric pattern.*

**Tonal analysis** *Everything – walls, woodwork, floor and fabrics – are in the same light tone.*

**Solution** *Make sure walls or floors are slightly lighter or darker, and introduce a little tonal contrast as an accent.*

# COLOUR AND PROPORTION

Learn how to use colours — warm or cool, light or dark — to change the shape and feel of a room.

The way you use colour on the six main areas of a room — the four walls, the floor and the ceiling — can dramatically or subtly alter the apparent proportions of the room. You can change how long a room looks, or how narrow or low it is, simply by the way you use colour and tone.

First, you need to give the room in question a long hard look. Does it basically have good proportions, or do they leave something to be desired? Is the ceiling a bit too high or too low? Does the hall feel like a long dark tunnel? Is the floor space rather small? Does the room feel too large for the amount of furniture in it? Are there awkward or untidy features — such as a sloping ceiling or a recess — which break up the space in the room and make it feel cramped?

A dark floor covering defines the edges of a large room, making the floor appear smaller than it really is.

If the room is well proportioned, you will want to make sure that you use colour and tone to enhance its good qualities. If the room needs help, the whole range of colours, from light to dark tones, are the home decorator's best friend.

## CHARACTERISTICS OF COLOUR

A colour can make a surface appear closer or further away, and so look smaller or larger in comparison to another colour. Being aware of the visual effects of different colours and tones helps you to create the effect you want.

Cool colours, such as blue-green, blue or blue-lilac, tend to recede, pushing back the walls of a room and making it feel more spacious. Light colours recede too, and so using a pale cool colour creates the maximum illusion of space. Add a pale wall-to-wall carpet and you increase the sense of space even more, particularly if the skirting board is painted in a colour similar to the carpet.

In contrast, walls painted in warm or dark colours seem closer. Large rooms with high ceilings can often feel spacious and unwelcoming and so painting the walls and ceiling in warm restful tones helps create a cosier and more relaxing atmosphere.

◁ *Raising the roof*
*This scheme is limited to beiges, browns and greys, in subtle tones which range from dark to light. It shows clearly how tone can affect the shape and feel of a room. A light ceiling and floor increase the  eight of the room, and a soft mid-tone draws in the walls slightly. A dark cornice gives added definition.*

## ALTERING SPACE WITH COLOUR

In high ceilinged rooms, corridors or narrow rooms, you can change the proportions of the space by contrasting dark floor and ceiling colours with light walls. This has the effect of appearing to lower the ceiling and increase the width of the room. In the same way, a long room appears shorter if the end wall is a warm rich colour.

A room with a low ceiling may feel oppressive, but if the ceiling is a much lighter colour than the walls, the room appears to be taller. Make sure that the walls are the same colour right up to the ceiling, not just to picture rail level, for maximum effect.

Sometimes rooms are squeezed into awkward spaces, particularly in flats converted from houses designed for more spacious living. Sloping ceilings, for example, can make a room feel cramped, but by blending the awkward shape in with the walls, you open up the space. Similarly, a recess can be drawn into a room by painting it in a warm or dark colour.

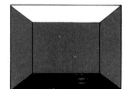

△ *Raising a ceiling*
*To make a ceiling feel higher, paint it in a lighter colour than the walls. In this rather box-shaped dining room the ceiling has been painted in brilliant white, in stark contrast with dark green walls. The light ceiling makes the room feel taller than it really is, and the dark tone draws the walls inwards, creating an intimate atmosphere.*

*It is important that the colour of the walls is continuous, right up to the height of the ceiling. If, for example, details such as the picture rail were picked out in another colour, breaking up the wall, the effect would not be so successful.*

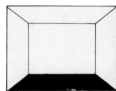

▷ *Making space*
*This is the same dining room as the one above, with the same furniture and carpet, but it looks completely different.*

*The walls and the ceiling are painted in soft pastel colours – a very light apricot and rose white. There is far less contrast between ceiling and walls than in the dark green dining room. Instead of appearing taller, the pale colours push the walls back and make the room feel larger and more light and airy. The cornice and picture rail are picked out in a slightly darker shade, to add definition.*

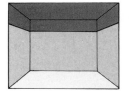

## ▷ Lowering a ceiling

Some rooms have ceilings which feel uncomfortably high for the size of the room. Painting the ceiling in a tone which is slightly darker than the walls makes it appear to be lower. The effect is increased if the ceiling colour is taken down to the level of the picture rail.

In this living room the problem is solved by painting the ceiling a dark ochre. Using the ceiling colour to outline the wall panels anchors the paler walls against the dark ceiling, at the same time balancing a colour scheme which could have been oppressive.

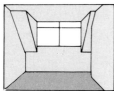

## △ Disguising awkward shapes

Attic rooms such as this one feel poky because a sloping ceiling creates awkward spaces. When decorating it's hard to know where the walls end and the ceiling begins: the ceiling will seem very low if the wallcovering ends where the slope begins. The best approach is to paint or paper the walls and ceiling in the same colour to camouflage the awkward shape. In this room mini-print wallpaper covers all the wall surfaces.

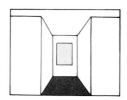

## ▷ Widening a narrow room

Corridors, galley kitchens, and small single bedrooms tend to be narrow, but if painted in very pale colours they appear more spacious.

The all-white fitted cupboards and appliances create an illusion of space in this narrow kitchen. The white venetian blind over the window blends the window into the wall when closed adding to this illusion. Bright red and white spotted tiles add interest to the white decoration.

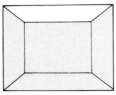

◁ **Making a room feel larger**
Pale colours reflect more light than dark colours, and cool colours recede. So a combination of the two is perfect for making a small room seem larger.

In this sunny little room, the walls, ceiling and floor are decorated in a range of cool pastels, creating a bright spacious airiness. Note that there are no great contrasts between colours to break up the overall effect. The woodwork of the window and the skirting boards are painted in pale aqua colours and the wooden floor is sanded and stained.

In a room that doesn't get any sun, temperate colours — such as pale lemon-yellow or pale lilac-grey — would be a better choice. A wall-to-wall carpet in a soft neutral colour is another way to add to the illusion of space, particularly if the skirting boards are painted in a similar colour. A neat window treatment, such as this roman blind, helps to keep the room uncluttered and spacious.

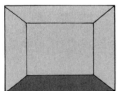

▷ **Making a large room cosier**
Spacious rooms can sometimes feel austere and unwelcoming, particularly if they get little sun. So, choose a tone from the warm side of the colour wheel — for both the ceiling and walls — to create a cheerful colour scheme which draws the walls inwards slightly and the ceiling downwards, making the room feel more inviting. The strength of the tone is as important as the colour itself, so use soft mid-tones for the best results. This large well-proportioned bedroom is painted in a soft rose pink to create a comfortable and restful atmosphere. The pink is warm enough to make the room feel cosier but not so strong that it becomes oppressive.

## THE IMPORTANCE OF TONE

It's hard to notice the tonal relationships of colours when looking at coloured photographs of rooms. But it's the way in which light, medium or dark tones are used that affects the shape of a room, even more than the actual colours themselves.

These diagrams show at a glance how to achieve a range of different effects, highlighting points you like and disguising problems. If you make a tracing of this page you can colour in the drawings to see how a variety of different colours – and different tones – look.

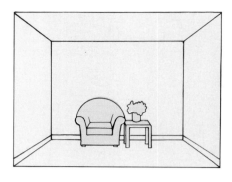

*To make a room feel larger* decorate in light colours. The lighter the colour the more light is reflected and the larger the room feels.

*To make a large room feel smaller* or cosier, use warm colours to bring the walls inwards and the ceiling downwards.

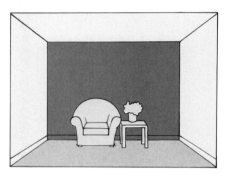

*Dark colours and warm colours* advance. A single wall painted in a dark colour will be drawn into the room.

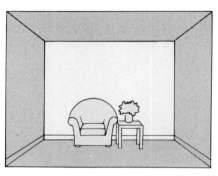

*Cool colours recede.* A wall painted in a light cool colour appears further away than it really is.

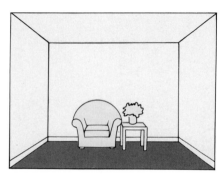

*A dark floorcovering* makes the floor seem smaller. It also defines the edges of the room and draws the eye downwards.

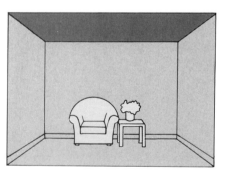

*To lower a ceiling* use a colour which is slightly darker than the walls but not so dark that it feels oppressive.

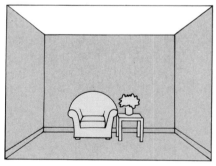

*To raise a ceiling* use a colour which is lighter than the walls. Increase the effect by painting the walls right up to the level of the ceiling.

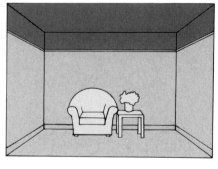

*To lower a ceiling in a very large room* paint the top section of the walls in the same dark colour as the ceiling.

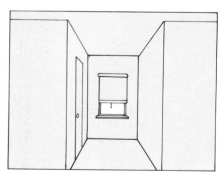

*To widen a corridor* use a very light colour on the walls, ceiling and floor. The reflected light will make the space seem less confined.

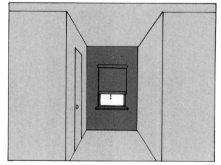

*To shorten a corridor,* or a long narrow room, paint the end wall in a dark or warm colour, to make it appear closer.

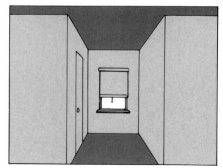

*To change the proportions* of a corridor, decorate the ceiling and floor in a darker colour than the walls. The space will appear wider and lower.

# THE EFFECT OF LIGHT ON COLOUR

When planning a colour scheme, it's important to know how natural and artificial lighting affect furnishings.

Professional interior designers and colour consultants consider the direction a room faces. Whether it is north, south, east, or west, makes a great deal of difference to the choice of colour scheme. For instance, a bedroom that faces east and receives strong sunlight in the early morning will look very different when next seen late at night in artificial lighting. A west-facing room that has a warm glow in the evening can look dull in the mornings. Your choice of colour should take this into account.

Of course, an ideal aspect is not always possible for everyone. City flats may enjoy little naturally-available light and be overlooked on all sides. A north-facing room can expect less sun than a south- or west-facing one; but whatever the aspect, with clever lighting and colour scheming the interior can be made to feel welcoming and attractive.

The style of house you live in can also make a great deal of difference to the amount of available light in an interior. A country cottage may be in a superbly sunny location but have low ceilings and tiny windows which can make the interior feel dark and gloomy. Modern homes with spacious open-plan interiors and large picture windows will be even more affected by their aspect and seasonal changes. If there is a living room with a patio or conservatory attached which is used as an additional seating area during the summer but not in winter, the decor will have to be flexible enough to accommodate the changes.

For people in doubt over lighting and colour schemes some top interior designers suggest painting a room white before making a final colour choice. This is a good way to observe how changes in natural light affect an interior and helps you make the most of it when choosing a colour scheme. Interior designer David Hicks has recently incorporated every kind of domestic light fitting into his showroom so that clients can also see the effect of different kinds of artificial light on carpets, fabrics and wallpapers.

### Diffused, even light
*A room in typically diffused northern daylight: shadows are not too strong and the mainly pale neutral colour scheme with colourful accents makes the most of existing light conditions. However, at night under artificial light, colours may alter drastically.*

## MATCHING FURNISHINGS

The most usual way to colour match is to look at samples in the daylight. However, this doesn't enable you to judge the effect at home under artificial lighting conditions. Viewing samples under shop lights is also unsatisfactory as they mostly use colour-corrected fluorescent tubes resembling daylight. Neither type of light will give an idea of the average home's tungsten lighting with its distinctive yellow cast. Carpets and textured fabrics are particularly vulnerable to change from artificial lighting. Synthetic fabrics that match perfectly in daylight may no longer do so under artificial light.

**Fabric** The effect of artificial lighting on curtains is better seen if a sample metre of fabric is pleated and held upright; looking at lampshade fabrics lit from behind also gives a better idea.

**Paint** Window walls will appear darker as they only receive reflected light; ceilings always look darker than walls painted the same colour. If in doubt use a shade lighter than your first choice; once all the walls are painted they tend to appear darker than the paint sample on a card.

**Carpets** Put samples flat on the floor and move them around the room to see how different positions and lighting conditions can affect the colour.

### △ ▷ Lighting – day and night
*It's hard to believe that these two pictures are of the same living room. (Above) Natural daylight shows off the subtle, neutral colour scheme of white and bluish greys in this modern interior.*

*(Right) The same living room seen at night under artificial lighting. The yellow cast of tungsten lighting has turned the grey upholstery and carpet a yellow-beige and given the entire room a unifying, warm glow.*

### △ Daylight
*Choosing colours by daylight can work well for rooms mainly in daytime use. But successful daytime colour combinations may not work well at night.*

### △ Fluorescent
*Some colour-corrected fluorescents can give much the same effect as daylight. Other types of fluorescent have a cold, blue and harsh draining effect.*

△ *Tungsten*
*The lighting most commonly used in the home. This emphasizes the yellow-reds, so a coral and apricot colour scheme will look much more intense.*

△ *Tungsten-halogen*
*This has a much whiter light than pure tungsten and would benefit a neutral blue-grey colour scheme more as there is less colour distortion.*

◁ *Peaches and corals for warmth*
North-facing rooms need to feel cosy.
Although some primrose yellows may
take on a greeny tinge and bright reds
feel claustrophobic, soft, muted coral
shades can work well in sponged,
dragged or stippled paint techniques.
Apricot or peach curtains at a window
give a warm cast to white walls. A
Chinese carpet with a coral background
warms up the floor.

▽ *South-facing, cool neutrals*
A neutral colour scheme using cool
blue-greys works well in this situation.
White sheer curtains at the window
diffuse and filter strong sunlight and
protect upholstery and carpet from the
sun's rays.

## △ Cool blue mood

This room feels typically Mediterranean with its tiled floor and cool, blue colour scheme. Blue-lined curtains lend a cool cast to the walls.
In winter these curtains could be changed to a warm peachy print with peach linings; while loose covers in warm peaches and beige could transform this into a warm, cosy colour scheme.

## ▷ North-facing using neutrals

A semi-transparent blind cleverly provides privacy without blocking out too much daylight.
 The light tan soft leather seating looks warm while the neutral beige carpet and touches of coral in an abstract rug and picture also help to warm up this scheme.

**Adding light** A white gloss-painted ceiling is a wonderful light reflector and in a dark room can act like a mirror and significantly increase the amount of available light. However, gloss-painted ceilings *must* be perfect – free from paint drips and unsightly cracks and bumps as a high sheen also emphasizes less-than-perfect surfaces!

△ **North-facing but warm**
Although green is generally considered a *cool* colour, the pale yellow-green on these walls combines successfully with a warm cream ceiling and the muted pink of the upholstery.

▽ **South-facing – using neutrals**
Browns appear less sombre in a south-facing room because the yellow emphasis of sunlight brings out the red which is the basis for browns.
White walls also take on a creamy look.

# WORKING WITH PATTERN

## Using pattern needs as much careful consideration as using colour to achieve successful results.

The number of patterns available in wallpapers, fabrics and floorcoverings nowadays is enormous, ranging from simple geometrics and colourful spatter designs to formal florals. How to choose patterns and how to use them can be an awe-inspiring prospect, but once you have learned about the characteristics of different patterns, creating the atmosphere or style you want becomes easier.

Pattern is an essential ingredient in any room scheme. It plays a part in creating the style and in enhancing the colour scheme, whether it is used in small areas – cushions, decorative paper borders or tiles, for example – or over much larger areas such as wallcoverings, ceilings and floors.

The strength of pattern should not be underestimated. Designs in a single bold colour appear to be more striking and imposing than a plain surface painted in the same colour. In the same way, a rather delicate pale colour is given more life on a patterned surface.

Scale is an important consideration, too. Large-scale designs can be wasted on the walls of small rooms, for instance, particularly if the wallpaper has a motif which is cut off in awkward places; and small bright designs tend to look busy.

On the next two pages patterned materials are divided up into eight different categories to provide a guide to the vast range of designs available.

### Single colour
*Mixing all sorts of patterns together seems like a risky business, but relating them to each other by choosing designs in the same colour is one way of making a successful combination.*

# TYPES OF PATTERN

## Checks, stripes and trellis
These patterns are some of the oldest and most striking designs. There are hundreds of variations in all colours, which can be traditional or modern in style – checks can be simple black and white squares, gingham or tartan, for example. A touch of one of these simple patterns makes a good accent in plain colour schemes.

## Spots and spatters
These designs have a very modern feel to them. Spots can be regularly spaced or randomly printed, large or small. Spatter patterns imitate the effects of tiny droplets of paint splashed and dribbled across the wall. Strong colours can be mixed together to create lively and vibrant combinations.

## Floral
Patterns range from large-scale oriental designs and traditional chintzes to splashy watercolour designs and very simple modern prints. The more dense florals need to be used in large rooms, but the softer colours and looser designs suit most rooms. They look good combined with plains which draw out the tones of the design.

## Abstract
A collection of modern patterns used in wallpapers and fabrics. They have no recognizable motifs, such as flowers, plants or birds; instead, they are made up of random shapes – splodges, freehand zig-zags, torn paper shapes or combinations of crooked lines and gentle swirls of colour, for instance, in all sorts of colour combinations.

### Geometric
The designs are made up of shapes such as triangles, chevrons, diamonds and key patterns. They come in all sizes and combinations of colours to create different effects – a crisp tailored look can be made by using geometrics for wallcoverings and window dressings, for instance. These designs often work well with mini-prints and florals.

### Exotic
The designs are based on traditional patterns from all over the world – India, Asia, Africa, the Pacific and the Americas. Rich colours and textures are combined in bold patterns – stripes, geometric or floral designs, or simple images of people and animals. Chinese designs are in delicate colours; Indian and African patterns are dark and rich.

### Mini-print
Wallpaper and fabrics are available in a wide variety of colours and patterns, including flower sprigs, florals and geometrical shapes. They can have a traditional cottagey feel to them and are especially suitable for small rooms where it would be easy for a larger patterned wallcovering to be overwhelming.

### Textural
These designs are printed to imitate other materials, such as wood grain, and various paint effects including stippling, sponging, dragging, rag rolling or marbling, and fabrics, such as moiré silk. These patterns give large flat surfaces, particularly walls, more visual interest and a luxurious feel without being overpowering.

△ **Daisy pink**
A wallpaper and fabric design of Michaelmas daisies – a pattern created at the end of the 19th Century by the famous English designer William Morris – makes a cosy atmosphere in this living room without feeling overwhelming. A plain carpet provides a neutral background for the wealth of pattern and the deep pink cushions act as accents.

◁ **Floral tradition**
The small, rather old-fashioned floral design on the wallpaper and fabric looks light and airy in this pretty bedroom. The broderie anglaise trim adds to the traditional feel of the room.

## ALL-OVER PATTERN

It is difficult to imagine what a pattern will look like over a large area when you are working from a sample. The main points to consider are the colours in the pattern, the type of design and its size.

Small designs, such as flower sprigs in pastel tones, can disappear on the walls of a large room – some even look like plains or textures from a distance. On the other hand, a small but boldly-coloured geometric makes a strong impact – this may be just the effect you want in a large and unwelcoming room, but it could be oppressive in a small room.

The type of design also affects the style of a room. If you are looking for a period atmosphere, go for traditional florals, Regency stripes, or paint effects, such as marbling, not brightly coloured geometrics, spots or checks.

◁ **Blue all over**
This simple colour scheme mixes mid-blue with the warm natural tones of wood and cane. The room is large and light enough to take the large-scale paisley pattern on the walls and ceiling without feeling dark or cramped.

71

### △ Pastel patterns

The bed is the biggest piece of furniture in a bedroom, and so the bedcover is an important part of the decorating scheme, especially when using a single pattern throughout the room. The effect could easily be overpowering, if not carefully planned.

This large-scale check in soft pastels – blue, mauve, pink, orange and yellow – is used in matching fabrics and wallcovering. It is an unusual but refreshing colour scheme for a bedroom.

### ▷ Spots and stripes

The mini-print design (right) – in soft grey with spots of pastel tones – or the boldly coloured exotic stripe (left) – called ikat and based on the patterns created by American Indians – provide two very different bedroom colour schemes.

# USING PATTERN WITH PLAIN

With just one pattern as the focal point in a room, there is a wide choice of ways to use plain colours open to you.

If you feel unsure about mixing and matching fabric and wallpaper patterns, then using one design with accompanying plain colours is the best way of building up an attractive and individual room scheme. Varying shades of one colour, or two or even three different colours picked from the chosen pattern can be used on walls and floor, upholstery and curtains. The many choices open to you for both paint colours and plain-coloured fabrics leave plenty of leeway to create different moods according to personal preference.

Textures, too, can be varied: a shiny chintz that reflects the light, or a rough, knobbly tweed that absorbs it, can create quite different effects even when they are the same colour.

If the pattern is in the upholstery, plain curtains edged with one other colour from the design look smart and sophisticated. Alternatively, if it is the curtains that are patterned, pick one of the colours in a self-patterned material for upholstery, with contrast piping and cushions in the curtain fabric.

Painted walls can be given added interest; the technique known as dragging adds a depth to the colour, while the techniques of ragging and sponging allow the introduction of two complementary colour shades that can be picked to tone with the fabric pattern.

Another possibility, of course, is that you have chosen a strongly-patterned wallpaper and wish to keep it as the main feature in your room. In this case, pick out two of the main colours for plain, tailored curtains or blinds.

### Beige as background
*Striking modern upholstery fabric makes a bold statement on its own. A nubbly natural tweed rug covers wood flooring and the walls are subtly dragged in pale blue on cream to echo the colouring of the upholstery. An unusual touch is the coffee table, which has been covered in pale beige chevron-design fabric to blend with the seating. Walls and table in all-over pale blue would create a much cooler feel in the room. The floral accents pick up the pink in the fabric but could equally well echo the blue.*

## PICKING OUT THE COLOURS

To help you decide which colours to pick for individual treatment, it's a good idea to match up some paint samples to the different colours in the pattern. Cut them out and look at them against a neutral background.

A multi-coloured fabric gives you a huge variety of colours to choose from: first, the shades that match precisely those contained in the pattern; second, a range of pastel tones in the same colours to soften the overall room scheme; and third, darker shades.

Those colours which are most pleasing to you — either because of their vibrancy or their soothing nature — are the ones to pick out for cushions, carpet, or walls.

△ *Colourful choice*
*A really colourful curtain fabric offers a wide range of colour choice for other surfaces in the room. Here is a selection of some of the plain fabrics and paint colours that could successfully be used to accompany it.*

▷ *Bright and cheerful*
*Jazzy modern interpretation of a floral print draws the eye immediately to the window and the view beyond. Yellow walls keep up the cheerful feeling set by the bright curtains. Contrasting lavender-blue cushions pick up another of the colours within the pattern, while the grey carpet subtly reflects the mauvish tint.*

△ **Summertime blues**
Focusing on the blues, a cooler scheme is created by putting very pale blue on the walls but a richer blue on the floor.

△ **Springtime freshness**
Picking out two different colours – palest pink walls and a mossy green carpet – brings a touch of spring to the room.

△ **Reversing the scheme**
The muted design on the wall is echoed in the cream curtains, grey carpet and reverse contrast-piped cushions.

▷ The wallpaper and fabric samples used in the room above. A self-patterned cream weave adds an interesting texture.

## △ Bright and light

A deep blue background with a bright, multi-coloured floral design forms the basis for a unusual bedroom scheme. Echoing pastel tints on the sofa soften the overall effect. On the right are some of the shades that could be picked out of the pattern to use in a colour scheme. Different textures for upholstery and curtains or cushions result in a different effect.

# WAYS WITH MINI PRINTS

Some of the most versatile patterns are the tiny, all-over designs that are not only pretty but also make good camouflage.

Mini prints were in vogue as soon as the first printed wallpapers and fabrics appeared in the 18th century. Their almost doll's house scale suited the contemporary Georgian homes and their elegant furniture. The Victorians, too, favoured tiny, all-over sprigged designs and frequently used them to great effect. Towards the end of the 19th century, however, mini print popularity declined in favour of larger, bolder patterns.

It wasn't until the 1970s that overall mini prints really came back into fashion. Firms such as Laura Ashley started to introduce them in ranges of closely colour co-ordinated wallpapers and furnishing fabrics that were largely inspired by both 18th century and Indian wood-block designs. They included sprigs of flowers, widely-spaced motifs and trellis patterns.

These small, pretty prints allowed people who had never before dared to mix patterns in a room to try their hand at it with success. Tile manufacturers then followed suit by matching their ranges to wallpapers and fabrics so schemes could be completely co-ordinated. Carpet manufacturers completed the mini pattern revolution by introducing tiny all-over designs.

## HOW TO USE THEM

There is a practical aspect to decorating with mini prints. They are particularly successful at camouflaging unevenly plastered wall surfaces — small all-over patterns break up large areas by preventing the eye from concentrating on one spot and seeing the flaws. All-over mini patterned carpets are also excellent for rooms that get heavy wear, particularly hallways, as they tend not to show the dirt as easily as plain ones.

However, mini prints do need to be chosen with care. They can be overpowering if the colour contrast between background and pattern is too marked. Small patterns may also lose definition in a large room but can be more successful when used in combination with a larger scale print.

### Muted background

*The mini-printed paper here is highly reminiscent of 18th century style both in design and colouring. The muted beige background makes a gentle contrast in relation to the motif making the overall effect easy on the eye and a good backdrop for dark furniture.*

△ **Traditional blue and white**
*Mini prints blend well with traditional furnishings and suit older homes and small rooms particularly well. Mixing different designs together is easier if you stick to matching colours.*

▷ **Mixing two together**
*The small-scale print on this dado area combines most successfully with the same pattern in a paler version on the walls above. The effect given by the two is surprisingly different.*

## HOW TO CHOOSE

In a shop where all you have to choose from is a sample book, it can sometimes be difficult to imagine how large expanses of a small design will look on a wall or hanging at your window. Whenever possible, try to see a big piece of the wallpaper or fabric. Stand away from it, screwing up your eyes slightly to get the effect. Some shops have made choosing mini prints easier by covering large display panels which can be viewed at a distance.

On wide-spaced mini prints, that is those with large areas of background colour in between the motifs, the spaces themselves start becoming more important and even form their own patterns within the design.

Geometric designs need to be considered very carefully. If your walls are slightly askew, a mini-print of this kind tends to emphasize it – especially if the pattern contains stripes as well. A pretty, overall floral design, on the other hand, can help to disguise bumpy walls.

Mini prints whose colours are closer in tonal value tend to merge together, whereas high colour contrasts look busier and crisper. Spaced sprigs with contrasting tones look even more widely spaced than ever. Generally speaking, this type of design looks better in smaller room schemes where there's not too much furniture or clutter.

As a more modern alternative to creating a romantic atmosphere with pastel flower sprigs, look for more geometric designs. Some of these geometrics can perhaps be held within stripes as they give a more formal look. In common with sponging and stippling, mini prints can soften dramatic expanses of wall and window colour by giving a more muted, dappled impression. They can also be used to introduce strong colour into a scheme.

## TYPES OF MINI PRINT

Mini prints come in a variety of looks, styles and patterns. It's important to understand the different effects that can be created when the same pattern is viewed close to and from a distance of around two metres away.

△ *Dark and light*
*A fabric or wallpaper with a predominantly red background brings walls and windows closer; white backgrounds make areas feel comparatively light.*

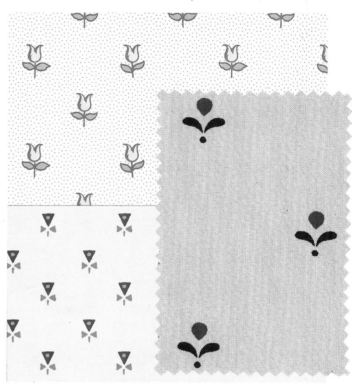

△ *Close together sprigs*
*Over large areas, widely-spaced designs can sometimes give a restless, 'dotted' effect whereas 'close together' prints can make small rooms feel claustrophobic.*

△ *Geometric*
*These prints can usefully offset fussy all-over mini floral patterns, giving the eye a break and making a mini print scheme feel more restful.*

△ *Contrast and close tones*
*Motifs in colours that are similar in tone to their backgrounds simplify complex, busy patterns and give a pleasantly muted effect to large expanses of wall or curtain.*

Prints here are two-thirds actual size

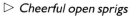

**△ Traditional geometric**
This Victorian-style mini print gives the impression of being light and lacy from a distance, but at close quarters it can be seen to be quite strong and dramatic.

**▷ Cheerful open sprigs**
A brightly contrasting striped print in red and white combined with a wide-spaced sprig pattern could be overpowering. However, the pale green leaves in the pattern bring relief by offsetting the sharp contrast. Adding a splash of deeper green plants makes the whole scheme feel more restful.

◁ △ *Patterned and plain*
*This bedroom's deep blue-green wallpaper is broken up by the overall design of twining white flowers (see detail). A colourful patchwork tablecloth echoes the floral mini print design, while plain blinds and curtains offset any busy feeling.*

▽ *Pattern for camouflage*
*All-over prints can help to disguise odd corners, awkward angles and uneven surfaces often found in older homes. Co-ordinating fabrics on the bed and at the window help to give a unified feel.*

# TAKING THE ROUGH WITH THE SMOOTH

Learn how to use textures – rough or smooth, matt or shiny, hard or soft – to bring life to your colour schemes.

Texture describes how any material feels to the touch. Every surface has a texture. If you compare, for example, the surfaces of a telephone and a kettle you will find that although both appear to be smooth they have quite different textures. The plastic has a warm feel to it, and is slightly brittle, but the metal of the kettle is cold and hard.

Texture can be visual as well as something you can feel. Painting techniques such as stippling, sponging, dragging or rag rolling create interesting visual textures on a smooth surface.

Deciding on which textures to use is as important a part of decorating as choosing colours because texture has as much effect on the different elements in a room and the overall atmosphere. A haphazard collection of textures can be as unsuccessful as an unbalanced colour scheme, so think carefully about the materials you plan to use and the surfaces – walls, floor, ceiling, furnishings – you are going to cover.

## CHOOSING TEXTURES

Textures are loosely divided into two groups – rough and smooth – which provoke quite different reactions. Rough textures, such as brick, wood, coir matting, wickerwork or suede, have a rustic homely feel about them. At the opposite extreme, the smoothness of glass, the hardness of chrome and the glossiness of plastic, for instance, bring a hard-edged look to a room.

You can create successful schemes using mixtures which are at neither one extreme nor the other. It's similar to mixing several different tones of one colour rather than just using dark or light ones.

Texture is also used in the same way as accents of colour. In a well-balanced but perhaps slightly boring colour scheme you can inject a little interest by adding a contrasting texture. Similarly, if a whole room is decorated using smooth textures, the addition of some rougher surfaces makes a lively contrast.

## HOW TEXTURE AFFECTS COLOUR

Texture is linked closely to colour. The quality of a colour – its richness or brightness, for instance – varies depending on the texture of the surface.

Smooth surfaces reflect light and dull ones absorb it. So the colour painted in emulsion on a wall looks lighter than the same colour used in a heavy woven fabric. Compare for yourself two objects in the same colour which have different textures – a red towel and a red plastic soap dish, for example – and you will see how the colour is affected.

### Combining textures
*This living room combines textures of all kinds. The shiny, polished chrome contrasts dramatically with the heavy, rugged tweed cover on the sofa. Suede chair covers, cotton drapes and a berber carpet add less extreme textures.*

## WALLS

The walls of a room are the largest surface area to decorate and there are literally thousands of different ways of treating them. Wallpapers, paints, fabrics and tiles all provide a wide selection of different textures.

Wallpapers are available in all kinds of finishes which range from smooth and gleaming foils to rich flocks and include embossed papers, such as anaglypta or woodchip, and vinyls which imitate textures such as moiré or raw silk; and real fabrics, such as hessian, wool, silk, linen, or cork.

Paints come in several finishes, too — silk or matt emulsion for walls, and gloss or eggshell for woodwork. There are plenty of painting techniques which add visual texture to the surface of a wall but are less overpowering than a tangible texture such as hessian or anaglypta. Rag-rolling creates an effect like soft, crushed silk, stippling looks like the texture of orange peel, and sponging, using two or three colours, can produce a wide range of mottled effects.

## WINDOWS

The texture of window dressings, whether they are curtains with swags and tails, or mirror venetian blinds, play an important part in creating the atmosphere of a room. Fabrics with a deep pile, such as velvet, suggest warmth; the sharp outline of a venetian blind has a cool businesslike quality to it; a neatly folding roman blind in cotton comes somewhere between the two.

The choice ranges from rich velvets to light, billowing sheers — and can include materials like muslin or felt.

The texture of window dressings is more pronounced because light not only shines on them but through them, too. The texture can be enhanced by the way the fabric is hung. Pleating or ruching, for example, creates a play of light and shadow on the surface of the fabric.

You don't have to limit yourself to one fabric at a window. Layers of different texture and pattern can be combined — a roller blind with curtains, two or three curtains of different weights, or draped fabric with blinds. The layers — say, lace, cotton and satin — are drawn back in stages to show off the different textures.

## FLOORS

The floor is the surface we are in most contact with and so the texture of the floor surface – whether it feels rough or smooth, warm or cold, hard or soft – is as important as the choice of colour and any practical considerations.

Carpets can be smooth, knobbly, sculpted, or flecked to create visual texture; rugs, rush, coir or sisal matting, wood or cork flooring all have a warm feel to them; quarry tiles, ceramic tiles, marble and slate are hard cool surfaces.

The floor is frequently the starting point for a decorating scheme. Using several different materials, wall-to-wall carpet, coir matting, wood and quarry tiles, perhaps, would make the overall effect in a house more interesting than if the same material had been used throughout.

In houses where rooms have more than one function, a change in the texture of the flooring can indicate the different uses of the space. For example, a kitchen/dining room could be laid with quarry tiles, with a floor rug under the table and chairs to bring warmth to the area which does not need to be so functional.

## OTHER SURFACES

Apart from the walls, floors and windows, there are many other surfaces to consider in a decorative scheme.

Furniture can combine all kinds of textures. Wood is a very versatile surface. Wooden furniture can be shiny and highly polished, or smooth with a matt finish, bleached, or pickled to bring out the grain, stained with a satin finish, or waxed to produce a subtle lustre or a hard glossy shine.

Wood laminates which are smooth and hardwearing are good for use in the kitchen. Other plastic laminates with a variety of surfaces – smooth, satin and matt stripes, marble effect, for example – are used for kitchen worktops, too.

Sofas and chairs can be covered in any number of furnishing fabrics ranging from nubbly tweeds, ribbed velvets, linen, glazed cottons, to leather and suede. Cane and rush seats are combined with wood or contrasted with chrome and cane furniture provides an alternative to wood.

Hard smooth surfaces such as glass and chrome create strong contrasts when combined with softer furnishing fabrics, but add to the smooth high-tech feel of leather, studded rubber or stainless steel.

## NATURAL TEXTURES

The nubbly surface of a berber carpet, the roughness of unpolished wood or cork, the softness of woollen fabrics are just a few of the natural textures which help to create a warm homely atmosphere in a room.

In the inviting interior shown above a limited range of colours – beige, terracotta, cream and white – and the lack of any strong pattern, show off the variety of surface textures. The smooth finish to the nest of pale oak tables, the picture frames and the painted wood panelling, complement the rough surface of the coir matting, the wool weave cover on the sofa and the glazed cotton cushions.

Notice how there are no extreme contrasts between textures. The coir matting has a herringbone pattern which adds interest to a plain scheme without dominating it by being too strong. In the same way, the wood, although highly polished, does not have the cold hardness of metals such as brass or stainless steel.

The combination of real textures, some rougher than others, and visual textures – such as the grain of the wooden picture frames and the oak tables – is successful because it is well balanced, creating a comfortable feel to the room. Lighting is important here too. A soft light enhances the differences between surface textures.

△ **Rough and ready**
*Pale cream wool weave, dark peach glazed cotton, coir matting and polished maple and oak make a comfortable mixture of real and visual textures.*

## SMOOTH SURFACES

Chrome, glass, marble, mirror, brass, ceramic and stainless steel are just some of the materials which have very hard, smooth surfaces. But not all very smooth surfaces are hard; materials, such as Perspex, vinyl, plastic laminates and leather, can have some flexibility in them, too.

Smooth textures can be shiny or matt: most shiny finishes, such as chrome, brass and mirror have a cold feel; in contrast, most matt surfaces, such as vinyl, stained wood or painted emulsion walls have some warmth in them.

A room which is made up entirely of smooth materials tends to have a hard-edged, even austere look to it. The dining room shown here is decorated with a variety of materials with smooth surfaces – chrome, perforated metal, vinyl, glass and stained wood – using a limited range of colours. The strong contrast between the colours – the black of the stained wood table and the white walls, for example – emphasizes the surface textures. The simple lines of the furniture bring this out, too. Look at the straight lines, sharp angles and geometric shapes, such as the glass and chrome side-tables shaped like cubes. The checked pattern of the vinyl floor makes an ideal background for this hard-edged linear scheme – although the effect is slightly softened by the use of grey rather than black with white.

△ *Going to extremes*
*Polished chrome, glass, g  zed china and vinyl combine matt and shiny finishes on smooth surfaces to give a hard-edged look.*

## FUNCTIONAL BUT COMFORTABLE

A combination of rough and smooth textures make a well-balanced room scheme. Practicality often plays a part. A deep pile carpet might seem perfect for a bathroom – warm and luxurious – but it's not very practical when there's a lot of water about. A lino or vinyl floor is a good alternative because it is waterproof, but a well-sealed cork floor would be better still, because it is both practical and warm to the touch.

A kitchen needs to be practical but it doesn't have to be high-tech. This kitchen achieves a balance between warm, homely textures – such as wood and cotton – and functional, hardwearing surfaces. The cupboards and work surfaces are finished in smooth white melamine with pale turquoise glazed wall tiles. The floor which looks fresh and is easy to clean, is painted in a matching blue with a white border and topped with a striped rug, which adds some warmth to the smooth floor without being impractical.

A simple cotton curtain hangs from a wooden pole above the stripped wood window frame. Notice that a roller blind in a contrasting fabric has been fitted as well. A rustic touch is added with the smooth stripped pine kitchen chairs and table covered with a finely woven white cloth with a pretty but simple lacy border.

△ *Rough and smooth*
*Polished wood, a rag-rug, crisp lace and china with a pretty floral design combine with hard-wearing, smooth melamine and a shiny glazed tile.*

# MIX-AND-MATCH PATTERNS

## Mixing several patterns together successfully in one room is now much simpler than it used to be.

Until recently, mixing patterns together in a room scheme needed an excellent eye for colour and self-confidence to carry through ideas. Co-ordinating a striped wallpaper with floral fabric and all the attendant accessories, meant trailing round the shops with cuttings, hoping that your purchase would be a faithful match to the original sample.

These days, more and more manufacturers are producing comprehensive mix-and-match ranges of fabric, wallpapers, borders – even trimmings.

These ranges allow for the creation of much more exciting room schemes without the risk of a disaster because they are intended to harmonize, even though the designs vary. They can include floral patterns, spots, stripes and plain colours – very often with a 'moiré' look or self-patterned weave in an upholstery weight fabric.

△ **Sample board**
Fabric and wallpaper samples used to build up the room scheme on the left.

◁ **Background link**
This warm beige background to the main pattern of apricot and blue flowers has a 'moiré-look' design. This is repeated on the wallpaper, which also echoes the apricot flowers. The table is covered with two cloths, both with a self-pattern. The top one is spotted and the bottom one has a moiré design to tie up with the overall theme.

### △ Geometrics

Four different zig-zag designs of muted neutrals combine to make a strikingly modern bedroom scheme. The vertical saw-tooth pattern on the walls is echoed in the zig-zags of the bedlinen and adjoining wall, and the more intricate herringbone on the reverse of the duvet cover introduces a lighter element into the overall picture while maintaining the geometric theme.

### ◁ Trellis and flowers

A bright geometric trellis design forms a natural background to a floral pattern which employs the same colours. Although two quite different styles of design, this combination works successfully because of the association of flowers with trelliswork and because the two principal colours are an exact match, coming from the manufacturer's same range. The small repeat of the trellis in the wallpaper border breaks up the large expanse of wall.

## PLANNING A SCHEME

When choosing a co-ordinated room scheme where all the design elements come from one range, first decide which pattern is likely to be needed in the largest amount. In most cases this is the wallpaper and the curtain fabric.

When considering the walls, there are further decisions to be made before your final choice. For example, will you need two wallpapers – above and below a chair rail, perhaps? Would you like to use a border – either to emphasize an architectural feature or to break up a featureless expanse?

With this settled you can then turn to the trimmings, details and finishing touches. If the curtains are long, would tiebacks enhance their appearance? If so, pick the same fabric or choose a blending one in a smaller design, and plan to repeat this in cushions or perhaps a tablecloth. If you want to dress the windows even more elaborately, consider adding a blind to match the tiebacks; there might, too, be a place for a window seat. Plain upholstery can be contrast-piped.

△ **Building up**
Lightly-patterned wallpaper of scattered leaves is topped by a more elaborate border – used again, but in reverse, above the picture rail. Colours in the curtain fabric are stronger, making them the dominating feature in the room.

Picking out the picture rail and coving in a paint that matches the colour of the wallpaper motif not only turns it into an interesting feature in its own right but is also a useful device for visually lowering the room height.

◁ **Eye-catching abstract**
Two vivid abstract designs can still harmonize because they contain the same colours and tones. Here, the pale straw background is repeated in the carpet, forming a soft, neutral contrast to the busy fabrics.

### △ Mini prints
The common denominator here is the all-over wallpaper design of small sprigged flowers, which is repeated and then over-printed with larger, stronger-coloured flowers in the fabric used for both blind and window seat. This gives emphasis to the window so that it is separated from, yet blends well with, the walls.

### ▷ Checks and flowers
All-in-all, there are five different patterns, from geometrical checks and stripes to a large floral design and a leafy mini print, blending in to make this harmonious bedroom scheme. This scheme works because all the fabrics come from the same dye lot. The pastel tones impart a quiet air to what could have been a busy mixture of design and colour.

△ **Sample board**
Samples of the five linked designs in the room shown left.

△ **Sophisticated country**
Rich raspberry self-patterned chintz forms a perfect backdrop to old wood, while the flowery cushions echo the furniture's country feel. The designs are held together by rich pink, which appears throughout, and the three-berry motif on both wallpapers and floral cushion covers.

▷ **Simply elegant**
An elegant little breakfast corner has been created by keeping to two colours – blue and white – and two motifs – flower sprigs and tiny spots. The simple chairs and dresser are painted and the dresser doors covered in the wallpaper.

## HOW TO BUILD UP A MIX-AND-MATCH SCHEME

Taking a window feature as an example, the illustrations show how an overall co-ordinated room scheme can be built up. Start with walls and drapes, then add festoons and a window seat, and finally the finishing touches of wallpaper border and cushions. Samples of the fabrics and papers used in the scheme are shown below.

△ **Stage 1** – Co-ordinating wallpaper and curtains are chosen hung and draped, with matching tiebacks.

△ **Stage 2** – A third co-ordinating design is added for festoon blinds and trimly-piped cushions placed in the window alcove.

△ **Stage 3** – Cushions introduce a fourth design, echoed in the border that neatly skirts the edge of the wallpaper.

# INDEX

PHOTOGRAPHIC CREDITS
Front cover Arthur Sanderson and Sons Ltd, 1 Coloroll, 2-3 Dulux, 4-5 Sara Taylor/Eaglemoss, 6 Arthur Sanderson and Sons Ltd, 7 Jerry Tubby/Eaglemoss, 9 Sara Taylor/Eaglemoss, 10 Syndication International/Ideal Home, 12(t) National Magazine Co/David Brittain, 12(b) Texas Homecare, 14 Camera Press/IMS, 15 Arthur Sanderson and Sons Ltd, 16 Designers Guild, 17 & 18 John Suett/Eaglemoss, 19 Dulux, 21 Coloroll, 23 Next Interior, 24 Dulux, 31 Simon Butcher/Eaglemoss, 32 National Magazine Co/David Brittain, 33 PWA International, 34 Next Interior, 35 Arthur Sanderson and Sons Ltd, 37 Dulux, 38(t) Syndication International/Ideal Home, 38(b) PWA International, 39(t) EWA/Michael Dunne, 39(b) Habitat, 40(t) Cover Plus from Woolworth, 40(b) PWA International, 41(t) Cover Plus from Woolworth, 41(b) National Magazine Co/David Brittain, 42 John Suett/Eaglemoss, 43 EWA/Michael Dunne, 44(t) Dulux, 44(b) Syndication International/Homes and Gardens, 45 Arthur Sanderson and Sons Ltd, 46(t) Syndication International/Ideal Home, 46(b) Crown Paints, 48 Crown Paints, 49 Habitat, 51 Hazel Digby/Eaglemoss, 52-3 Next Interior, 55 Osborne and Little, 56 Dulux, 57(t) Cover Plus from Woolworth, 57(b) Dulux, 58(t) PWA International, 58(b) EWA/Spike Powell, 59(t) Jerry Tubby/Eaglemoss, 59(b) Michael Boys, 61 Casa Viva, 62 & 63 EWA/Clive Helm, 64(t) EWA/Michael Nicholson, 64(b) Habitat, 65 Dulux, 66(t) Ken Kirkwood, 66(tr) EWA/Spike Powell, 66(b) EWA/Clive Helm, 67 Paper Moon Ltd, 70 EWA/Michael Dunne, 71(t) Arthur Sanderson and Sons Ltd, 71(b) EWA/Michael Dunne, 72 Habitat, 73 EWA/Michael Dunne, 74 Swish Products Ltd, 76 Dorma, 77 National Magazine Co/Jan Baldwin, 78 Syndication International/Woman and Home, 79 Crown Wallcoverings, 81(t) EWA/Di Lewis, 81(b) Crown Wallcoverings, 82(t) EWA/Spike Powell, 82(b) Vymura International, 83 EWA/Michael Dunne, 84 & 85 Sara Taylor/Eaglemoss, 86 National Magazine Co/David Brittain, 87 Camera Press, 88 Schreiber, 89 Arthur Sanderson and Sons Ltd, 90(t) Coloroll, 90(b) Interior Selection, 91(t) Interior Selection, 91(b) Collier Campbell, 92(t) EWA/Di Lewis, 92(b) Jerry Tubby/Eaglemoss, 93(t) Bryan Yates, 93(b) The Picture Library